This item has to be renewed or returned on or before
the last date below

TWO WEEK LOAN

D0581270

LONGMAN

Post-1914 Stories from other Cultures

Angelou, Goodison, Senior & Walker   *Quartet of Stories*   0 582 28730 8
Nadine Gordimer   *July's People*   0 582 06011 7
Ruth Prawer Jhabvala   *Heat and Dust*   0 582 25398 5
Alan Paton   *Cry, the Beloved Country*   0 582 07787 7
selected by Madhu Bhinda   *Stories from Africa*   0 582 25393 4
                                         Stories from Asia   0 582 03922 3
selected by B Naidoo, C Donovan, A Hicks   *Global Tales*   0 582 28929 7

Post-1914 Non-Fiction

selected by Geoff Barton   *Genres*   0 582 25391 8
selected by Celeste Flower   *Diaries and Letters*   0 582 25384 5
selected by Peter Griffiths   *Introducing Media*   0 582 28932 7
selected by Linda Marsh   *Travel Writing*   0 582 25386 1˙
                                   Autobiographies   0 582 08837 2

                    The Diary of Anne Frank   0 582 01736 X

Pre-1914 Fiction

Jane Austen   *Pride and Prejudice*   0 582 07720 6
Charlotte Brontë   *Jane Eyre*   0 582 07719 2
Emily Brontë   *Wuthering Heights*   0 582 07782 6
Charles Dickens   *Great Expectations*   0 582 07783 4
                        Oliver Twist   0 582 28729 4
                        A Christmas Carol   0 582 23664 9
George Eliot   *Silas Marner*   0 582 23662 2
Thomas Hardy   *The Mayor of Casterbridge*   0 582 22586 8
                        Far from the Madding Crowd   0 582 07788 5
Edith Wharton   *Ethan Frome*   0 582 30244 7

Contents

CONTENTS

 Introduction

What right have we to read the personal diaries and correspondence of others? Are we behaving like voyeurs, prying into the lives of others when we do so? This collection brings together some of the intimate writing of people from the past and the present.

Most diaries are not intended for the eyes of anyone other than the writer. There is still a sense of taboo about reading another's diary. Yet diaries can provide historians and sociologists with valuable information, give literary enthusiasts an insight to writers, and political scientists a perspective beyond parliamentary records. Meanwhile they are an enjoyable read.

Diaries are daily records of events, experiences, emotions and thought processes, shopping lists and sums. Although not usually intended for publication, the diary may be written for more than just the diarist's enjoyment. William Wordsworth actively encouraged his sister's journal. Others represented in this collection were invited to publish their journals and set to editing what they had written to make it accessible to a general reader (Fanny Burney, Alan Clark and Zlata Filipovic are among these). Diarists' styles range from the shorthand to the elaborate.

Letter writers take their reader into account from the first stroke of the pen. Exchanges of letters can prove very interesting to read although replies to letters have not been included here. Letters are as varied in style as diaries, reflecting the personality of the writer and, in many ways, the recipient too. Letters written at leisure will have a different tone to those written hurriedly.

Diaries and letters might be thought of as written when their authors are 'off-duty'. The collection here shows that even off-duty writers employ their very best written styles at all times, and can be more incisive, more critical and even more humorous when in informal mode. The diary extracts and letters given are tasters of the wider collections available from some of the writers. They can also be regarded as a unified set of materials for study and comparison. The study activities are intended to help you find your way into and around the diaries and letters; you might even decide to attempt the first of these before you begin your reading.

Celeste Flower

Presenting Bungay

Sir John Harington

Sir John Harington (1561–1612) was a godson of Elizabeth I, a courtier and a wit. He wrote and translated works written by others throughout his life, and was inventive enough to produce a design for a prototype WC. This letter is to Prince Henry, the eldest son of James I, who at the time is about fourteen years old. Kelston is near Bath.

14 June 1608   *Kelston*

May it please your Highness: having good reason to think your Highness has good will and liking to read what others have told of my rare Dogge, I will even give a brief history of his good deeds and strange feats; and herein will I not play the cur[1] myself, but in good sooth relate what is no more nor less than bare verity. Although I mean not to disparage the deeds of Alexander's horse,[2] I will match my Dogge against him for good carriage, for, if he did not bear a great Prince on his back, I am bold to say he did often bear the sweet words of a greater Princess[3] on his neck.

I did once relate to your Highness how he did sojourn from my house at Bath to Greenwich Palace, and deliver up to the Court there such matters as were entrusted to his care. This he hath often done, and

[1] play the scoundrel – a pun on the word 'cur' for dog
[2] Alexander the Great's horse, Bucephalus
[3] Elizabeth I

came safe to Bath or my house here at Kelston, with goodly returns from such Nobility as were pleased to employ him; nor was it ever told our Lady Queen that this Messenger did ever blab aught concerning his high trust, as others had done in more special matters.

Neither must it be forgotten how he once was sent with two charges of sack wine[4] from Bath to my house, by my man Combe; and on his way the cordage did slacken; but my trusty bearer did now bear himself so wisely as to covertly hide one flasket in the rushes, and take the other in his teeth to the house; after which he went forth, and returned with the other part of his burden to dinner. Hereat your Highness may perhaps marvel and doubt, but we have living testimony of those who wrought in the fields and espied his work, and now live to tell they did much want to play the Dogge and give stowage[5] to the wine themselves; but they did refrain, and watched the passing of the whole business.

I need not say how much I did once grieve at missing this Dogge; for on my journey towards London some idle pastimers did divert themselves with hunting mallards in a pond, and conveyed him to the Spanish Ambassador's, where, in a happy hour, after six weeks I did hear of him; but such was the court he did pay to the Don[6] that he was no less in good liking there than at home. Nor did the household listen to my claim or challenge till I rested my suit on the Dogge's own proofs, and made him perform such feats before the Nobles assembled, as to put it past doubt that I was his master. I did send him to the hall in the time of dinner, and made him bring thence a pheasant out of the dish, which created much mirth; but much more when he

[4] two loads of Spanish wine
[5] i.e. drink it themselves
[6] title of a Spanish nobleman, i.e. Sir

returned at my commandment to the table again and put it again in the same cover. Herewith the company was well content to allow my claim, and we both were well content to accept it, and come homewards.

I will now say in what manner he died. As we travelled towards Bath, he leaped on my horse's neck, and was more earnest in fawning and courting my notice than what I had observed for some time back, and after my chiding his disturbing my passing forwards, he gave me some glances of such affection as moved me to cajole[7] him; but alas, he crept suddenly into a thorny brake, and died in a short time.

Now let Ulysses praise his dogge Argus, or Tobit[8] be led by that dogge whose name doth not appear, yet could I say such things of my Bungay, for so was he styled, as might shame them both, either for good faith, clear wit, or wonderful deeds; to say no more than I have said of his bearing letters to London and Greenwich more than an hundred miles.

As I doubt not your Highness would love my Dogge, if not myself, I have been thus tedious in his story, and again say that of all the Dogges near your father's Court, not one hath more love, more diligence to please, or less pay for pleasing than him I write of; for verily a bone will content my servant, when some expect greater matters, or will knavishly find out a bone of contention.

I now rest your Highness's friend in all service that may suit him,

JOHN HARINGTON

[7] to pet, flatter
[8] Ulysses was a hero of Greek legend whose dog was the first to recognise him when he returned home from Troy after a ten-year odyssey; the story of Tobit is in the Apocrypha (see Tobit 5:16).

The King's War

King Charles I
Prince Rupert

Charles I (1600–49) was King of Great Britain and Ireland from 1625 to 1649. His rule was unpopular and led to Civil War. Charles was eventually executed by the Parliamentarians who opposed him. Prince Rupert (1619–82) was the son of Charles I's sister, Elizabeth of Bohemia. During the English Civil War he gained prowess as a cavalry leader. He was made General of Horse in 1642 and given chief command of the army two years later.

Both of these letters were written during the English Civil War. The first is from Charles to Rupert, and was written early in the morning before the Battle of Edgehill. The second is from Rupert to Colonel William Legge, asking for stores and ammunition for the Royalist forces in Shropshire. Langdale was a Royalist cavalry commander; Maurice was Rupert's younger brother.

23 October 1642

Nephew,

I have given order as you have desired; so I doubt not but all the foot and cannon will be at Edgehill betimes this morning, where you will also find

> Your loving uncle and faithful friend,
> CHARLES R.

4 o'clock this Sunday morning.

11 March 1645   *Ludlow*

Dear Will,

I have received but one despatch in return for three sent. Hasten the ammunition. I shall not want pike-heads; there are two thousand three hundred at Worcester. I must have stores or money. Sir Marmaduke Langdale, with the Northern Horse, is come to Bridgenorth. On Thursday we meet at Wellington; on Friday Rupert and Maurice will join, if possible, near Ellesmere. If this succeed, there will be more hopes left.

Dabscourt writes the powder is stopped in Monmouthshire, where they are associating against us, and will send no carriages. Therefore, you at Oxford must look to them. I am going about a nobler business; therefore pray God for me, and remember me to all my friends.

Your assured friend,
RUPERT

London Calamity

Samuel Pepys

Samuel Pepys (1633–1703) kept his diary from January 1660 to May 1669, covering an exciting period of change in English history. From him we learn much about London life during the reign of Charles II and gain valuable insight into some major events of the times. The diary itself was written in cipher, a kind of shorthand which was not fully understood until 1825.

The Great Fire of London broke out overnight on 2 September 1666 and spread rapidly through the old timber-framed buildings of the city. Hardly anyone died even though the fire raged for four days, destroying most of the city. Samuel Pepys's eye-witness account is famous.

2 September 1666

Lords Day.[1] Some of our maids sitting up late last night to get things ready against our feast today, Jane called us up, about 3 in the morning, to tell us of a great fire they saw in the City. So I rose, and slipped on my night-gown and went to her window, and thought it to be on the back side of Markelane at the furthest; but being unused to such fires as fallowed,[2] I thought it far enough off, and so went to bed again and to sleep. About 7 rose again to dress myself, and there looked out at the window and saw the fire not so much as it was,

[1] Sunday
[2] possibly 'followed'

and further off. So to my closet to set things to rights after yesterday's cleaning. By and by Jane comes and tells me that she hears that above 300 houses have been burned down tonight[3] by the fire we saw, and that it was now burning down all Fishstreet by London Bridge. So I made myself ready presently, and walked to the Tower and there got up upon one of the high places, Sir J. Robinson's little son going up with me; and there I did see the houses at that end of the bridge all on fire, and an infinite great fire on this and the other side the end of the bridge – which, among other people, did trouble me for poor little Michell and our Sarah on the Bridge. So down, with my heart full of trouble, to the Lieutenant of the Tower, who tells me that it begun this morning in the King's bakers house in Pudding Lane, and that it hath burned down St Magnes Church and most part of Fishstreete already. So I down to the water-side and there got a boat and through bridge, and there saw a lamentable fire. Poor Michell's house, as far as the Old Swan, already burned that way and the fire running further, that in a very little time it got as far as the Stillyard while I was there. Everybody endeavouring to remove their goods, and flinging into the river or bringing them into lighters that lay off. Poor people staying in their houses as long as till the very fire touched them, and then running into boats or clambering from one pair of stair by the waterside to another. And among other things, the poor pigeons I perceive were loath to leave their houses, but hovered about the windows and balconies till they were some of them burned, their wings, and fell down.

Having stayed, and in an hour's time seen the fire rage every way, and nobody to my sight endeavouring to

[3] last night

quench it, but to remove their goods and leave all to the fire; and having seen it get as far as the Steeleyard, and the wind mighty high and driving it into the city, and everything, after so long a drought, proving combustible, even the very stones of churches. I to Whitehall with a gentleman with me who desired to go off from the Tower to see the fire in my boat – to Whitehall, and there up to the King's closet in the chapel, where people came about me and I did give them an account dismayed them all; and word was carried in to the King, so I was called for and did tell the King and Duke of York what I saw, and that unless his Majesty did command houses to be pulled down, nothing could stop the fire. They seemed much troubled, and the King commanded me to go to my Lord Mayor from him and command him to spare no houses but to pull down before the fire every way. The Duke of York bid me tell him that if he would have any more soldiers, he shall. Here meeting with Captain Cocke, I in his coach, which he lent me, and Creed with me, to Pauls; and there walked along Watling Street as well as I could, every creature coming away loaden with goods to save – and here and there sick people carried away in beds. Extraordinary good goods carried in carts and on backs. At last met my Lord Mayor in Canning Streete, like a man spent,[4] with a hankercher about his neck. To the King's message, he cried like a fainting woman, 'Lord, what can I do? I am spent! People will not obey me. I have been pulling down houses. But the fire overtakes us faster than we can do it.' That he needed no more soldiers; and that for himself, he must go and refresh himself, having been up all night. So he left me, and I him, and walked home

[4] exhausted

– seeing people all almost distracted and no manner of means used to quench the fire. The houses too, so very thick thereabouts, and full of matter for burning, as pitch and tar, in Thames Street – and warehouses of oyle and wines and brandy and other things. Here I saw Mr Isaccke Houblon, that handsome man – prettily dressed and dirty at his door at Dowgate, receiving some of his brothers things whose houses were on fire; and as he says, have been removed twice already, and he doubts (as it soon proved) that they must be in a little time removed from his house also – which was a sad consideration. And to see the churches all filling with goods, by people who themselfs should have been quietly there at this time.

As soon as dined, I and Moone away and walked through the City, the streets full of nothing but people and horses and carts loaden with goods, ready to run over one another, and removing goods from one burned house to another – they now removing out of Canning Street (which received goods in the morning) into Lumbard Streete and further. We parted at Pauls, he home and I to Pauls Wharf, where I had appointed a boat to attend me; and took in Mr Carcasse and his brother, whom I met in the street, and carried them below and above bridge, to and again, to see the fire, which was now got further, both below and above, and no likelihood of stopping it. Met with the King and Duke of York in their barge, and with them to Queen Hith and there called Sir Rd. Browne to them. Their order was only to pull down houses apace, and so below bridge at the waterside; but little was or could be done, the fire coming upon them so fast. Good hopes there was of stopping it at the Three Cranes above, and at Buttolphs Wharf below bridge, if care be used; but the wind carries it into the City, so as we know not by the

waterside what it doth there. River full of lighters and
boats taking in goods, and good goods swimming in the
water; and only, I observed that hardly one lighter or
boat in three that had the goods of a house in, but
there was a pair of virginals[5] in it. Having seen as much
as I could now, I away to Whitehall by appointment, and
there walked to St James's Park, and there met my wife
and Creed and Wood and his wife and walked to my
boat, and there upon the water again, and to the fire up
and down, it still increasing and the wind great. So near
the fire as we could for smoke; and all over the Thames,
with one's face in the wind you were almost burned
with a shower of firedrops – this is very true – so as
houses were burned by these drops and flakes of fire,
three or four, nay five or six houses, one from another.
When we could endure no more upon the water, we to
a little alehouse on the Bankside over against the Three
Cranes, and there stayed till it was dark almost and saw
the fire grow; and as it grow darker, appeared more and
more, and in corners and upon steeples and between
churches and houses, as far as we could see up the hill
of the City, in a most horrid malicious bloody flame, not
like the fine flame of an ordinary fire. We stayed till, it
being darkish, we saw the fire as only one entire arch of
fire from this to the other side the bridge, and in a bow
up the hill, for an arch of above a mile long. It made me
weep to see it. The churches, houses, and all on fire and
flaming at once, and a horrid noise the flames made,
and the cracking of houses at their ruine. So home with
a sad heart, and there find everybody discoursing and
lamenting the fire; and poor Tom Hater came with
some few of his goods saved out of his house, which is
burned upon Fish Street Hill. I invited him to lie at my

[5] keyboard instrument

house, and did receive his goods; but was deceived in his lying there, the noise coming every moment of the growth of the fire, so as we were forced to begin to pack up our own goods and prepare for their removal. And did by mooneshine (it being brave, dry, and moonshine and warm weather) carry much of my goods into the garden, and Mr Hater and I did remove my money and iron chests into my cellar – as thinking that the safest place. And got my bags of gold into my office ready to carry away, and my chief papers of accounts also there, and my tallies into a box by themselfs. So great was our fear, as Sir W. Batten had carts come out of the country to fetch away his goods this night. We did put Mr Hater, poor man, to bed a little; but he got but very little rest, so much noise being in my house, taking down of goods.

3 September

About 4 a-clock in the morning, my Lady Batten sent me a cart to carry away all my money and plate and best things to Sir W. Rider's at Bednall Greene; which I did, riding myself in my nightgown in the cart; and Lord, to see how the streets and the highways are crowded with people, running and riding and getting of carts at any rate to fetch away things. I find Sir W. Rider tired with being called up all night and receiving things from several friends. His house full of goods and much of Sir W. Batten and Sir W. Penn's. I am eased at my heart to have my treasure so well secured. Then home, with much ado to find a way. Nor any sleep all this night to me nor my poor wife. But then, and all this day, she and I and all my people labouring to get away the rest of our things, and did get Mr Tooker to get me a lighter to take them in, and we did carry them (myself some)

11

over Tower Hill, which was by this time full of people's goods, bringing their goods thither. At night, lay down a little upon a quilt of W. Hewer in the office (all my own things being packed up or gone); and after me, my poor wife did the like – we having fed upon the remains of yesterday's dinner, having no fire nor dishes, nor any opportunity of dressing[6] anything.

4 September

Sir W. Batten, not knowing how to remove his wine, did dig a pit in the garden and laid it in there; and I took the opportunity of laying all the papers of my office that I could not otherwise dispose of. And in the evening Sir W. Penn and I did dig another and put our wine in it, and I my parmezan cheese as well as my wine and some other things.

This afternoon, sitting melancholy with Sir W. Penn in our garden and thinking of the certain burning of this office without extraordinary means,[7] I did propose for the sending up of all our workmen from Woolwich and Deptford yards (none whereof yet appeared), and to write to Sir W. Coventry to have the Duke of York's permission to pull down houses rather then lose this office, which would much hinder the King's business. So Sir W. Penn he went down this night, in order to the sending them up tomorrow morning.

This night Mrs Turner (who, poor woman, was removing her goods all this day – good goods, into the garden, and knew not how to dispose of them) – and her husband supped with my wife and I at night in the office, upon a shoulder of mutton from the cook's,

[6] preparing
[7] unless something exceptional were done about it

without any napkin or anything, in a sad manner but were merry. Only, now and then walking into the garden and saw how horridly the sky looks, all on a fire in the night, was enough to put us out of our wits; and endeed it was extremely dreadfull – for it looks just as if it was at us, and the whole heaven on fire. I after supper walked in the dark down to Tower Street, and there saw it all on fire at the Trinity House on that side and the Dolphin tavern on this side, which was very near us – and the fire with extraordinary vehemence. Now begins the practice of blowing up of houses in Tower Street, those next the Tower, which at first did frighten people more then anything; but it stopped the fire where it was done – it bringing down the houses to the ground in the same places they stood, and then it was easy to quench what little fire was in it, though it kindled nothing almost. W. Hewer this day went to see how his mother did, and comes late home, but telling us how he hath been forced to remove her to Islington, her house in Pye Corner being burned. So that it is got so far that way and all the Old Bayly, and was running down to Fleetestreete. And Pauls is burned, and all Cheapside. I wrote to my father this night; but the post-house being burned, the letter could not go.

A Journey across the English Channel

Lady Mary Wortley Montagu

Lady Mary Wortley Montagu (1689–1762) was a society hostess and famous letter-writer. She spent much time abroad, particularly in Turkey. There she found out about vaccination against smallpox and had it introduced to Britain on her return. Lady Mary has just returned to England from Turkey in a packet boat, which carried the mail as well as passengers. Her letter is written to an Italian literary man called the Abbé Conti, so he would be familiar with becafiguas, which are small birds eaten as a delicacy in Italy.

31 October 1718   *Dover*

I arrived this morning at Dover, after being tossed a whole night in the packet boat, in so violent a manner that the master, considering the weakness of his vessel, thought it prudent to remove the mail, and gave us notice of the danger. We called a little fisher boat, which could hardly make up to[1] us; while all the people on board us were crying to Heaven; and 'tis hard to imagine one's self in a scene of greater horror than on such an occasion; and yet, shall I own it to you? though I was not at all willing to be drowned, I could not forbear being entertained at the double distress of a fellow passenger. She was an English lady that I had met at Calais, who desired me to let her go over with me in

[1] come near

my cabin. She had bought a fine point-head,[2] which she was contriving to conceal from the custom-house officers. When the wind grew high, and our little vessel cracked, she fell very heartily to her prayers, and thought wholly of her soul. When it seemed to abate, she returned to the worldly care of her head-dress, and addressed herself to me:

'Dear Madam, will you take care of this point?[3] if it should be lost. – Ah, Lord, we shall all be lost! Lord have mercy on my soul! – Pray, madam, take care of this head-dress.'

This easy transition of her soul to her head-dress, and the alternate agonies that both gave her, made it hard to determine which she thought of greatest value. But, however, the scene was not so diverting but I was glad to get rid of it, and be thrown into the little boat, though with some hazard of breaking my neck.

It brought me safe hither; and I cannot help looking with partial eyes on my native land. That partiality was certainly given us by nature, to prevent rambling, the effect of an ambitious thirst after knowledge, which we are not formed to enjoy. All we get by it is a fruitless desire of mixing the different pleasures and conveniences which are given to different parts of the world, and cannot meet in any one of them.

After having read all that is to be found in the languages I am mistress of, and having decayed my sight by midnight studies I envy the peace of mind of a ruddy milkmaid, who, undisturbed hears the sermon with humility every Sunday. And, after having seen part of Asia, and Africa, and almost made the tour of Europe, I think the honest English squire more happy,

[2] lace head-dress
[3] lace

who verily believes the Greek wines less delicious than March beer; that the African fruits have not so fine a flavour as golden pippins; and the becafiguas of Italy are not so well tasted as a rump of beef; and that, in short, there is no perfect enjoyment of this life out of Old England. I pray God I may think so for the rest of my life; and, since I must be contented with our scanty allowance of daylight, that I may forget the enlivening sun of Constantinople.

I am,
Etc., etc.

Everyday Adventures and Awkward Moments

Fanny Burney

Fanny Burney (1752–1840) was born in Norfolk, the daughter of a musicologist. She was educated at home and spent many hours writing and reading. Her talents developed early and she wrote several novels and other works. She eventually became Madame D'Arblay, and her letters and diaries were published posthumously in 1846.

At the age of fifteen Fanny burned her existing writings but could not give up the habit of 'scribbling'. In the first extract, while visiting London, she resolves to keep a regular diary and considers the question of 'audience'. Later she gives us a taste of her lifestyle in Norfolk. She describes her reaction to a book she has been reading, the 'moral fable' *Rasselas: The Prince of Abyssinia* by Samuel Johnson. Then imagine her horror when one day she realises that she has carelessly left a page of her diary where her father can find it! (Miss Young is a family friend.)

27 March 1768   *Poland Street, London*

To have some account of my thoughts, manners, acquaintance and actions, when the hour arrives in which time is more nimble than memory, is the reason which induces me to keep a Journal. A Journal in which I must confess my *every* thought, must open my whole heart! But a thing of this kind ought to be addressed to somebody – I must imagine myself to be talking –

talking to the most intimate of friends – to one in whom I should take delight in confiding, and remorse in concealment: – but who must this friend be? to make choice of one in whom I can but *half* rely, would be to frustrate entirely the intention of my plan. The only one I could wholly, totally confide in, lives in the same house with me, and not only never *has*, but never *will*, leave me one secret to tell her. To *whom*, then, *must* I dedicate my wonderful, surprising and interesting Adventures? – to *whom* dare I reveal my private opinion of my nearest relations? my secret thoughts of my dearest friends? my own hopes, fears, reflections, and dislikes? – Nobody!

To Nobody, then, will I write my Journal! since to Nobody can I be wholly unreserved – to Nobody can I reveal every thought, every wish of my heart, with the most unlimited confidence, the most unremitting sincerity to the end of my life! For what chance, what accident can end my connections with Nobody? No secret *can* I conceal from Nobody, and to Nobody can I be *ever* unreserved. Disagreement cannot stop our affection, Time itself has no power to end our friendship. The love, the esteem I entertain for Nobody, Nobody's self has not power to destroy. From Nobody I have nothing to fear, the secrets sacred to friendship Nobody will not reveal when the affair is doubtful, Nobody will not look towards the side least favourable.

I will suppose you, then, to be my best friend, (tho' Heaven forbid you ever should!) my dearest companion – and a romantic girl, for mere oddity may perhaps be more sincere – more tender – than if you were a friend in propria persona[1] – in as much as imagi-

---

[1] in person, in real life

nation often exceeds reality. In your breast my errors may create pity without exciting contempt; may raise your compassion, without eradicating your love. From this moment, then, my dear girl – but why, permit me to ask, must a *female* be made Nobody? Ah! my dear, what were this world good for, *were* Nobody a female? And now I have done with preambulation.[2]

17 July   *Norfolk*

Such a set of tittle tattle, prittle prattle visitants! Oh dear! I am so sick of the ceremony and fuss of these fall lall[3] people! So much dressing – chit chat – complimentary nonsense – In short, a Country Town is my detestation – all the conversation is scandal, all the attention, dress, and *almost* all the heart, folly, envy, and censoriousness. A City or a village are the only places which I think, can be comfortable, for a Country Town, I think has all the bad qualities, without one of the good ones, of both.

We live here, generally speaking, in a very regular way – we breakfast always at 10, and rise as much before as we please – we dine precisely at 2, drink tea about 6 – and sup exactly at 9. I make a kind of rule, never to indulge myself in my two *most* favourite pursuits, reading and writing, in the morning – no, like a very good girl I give that up wholly, accidental occasions and preventions excepted, to needle work, by which means my reading and writing in the afternoon is a pleasure I cannot be blamed for by my mother, as it does not take up the time I ought to spend otherwise. I never pretend to be so superior a being as to be above having and

[2] introduction
[3] foppish, trifling

indulging a *Hobby Horse*,[4] and while I keep mine within due bounds and limits, nobody, I flatter myself, would wish to deprive me of the poor animal: to be sure, he is not form'd for labour, and is rather lame and weak, but then the dear creature is faithful, constant, and loving, and tho' he sometimes prances, would not kick anyone into the mire, or hurt a single soul for the world – and I would not part with him for one who could win the greatest prize that ever *was* won at any Races.

Alas, alas! my poor Journal! how dull unentertaining, uninteresting thou art! – oh what would I give for some Adventure worthy reciting – for something which would surprise – astonish you! I have lately read the Prince of Abyssinia – I am almost equally charm'd and shocked at it – the style, the sentiments are inimitable – but the subject is dreadful – and handled as it is by Dr Johnson, might make *any* young, perhaps old, person tremble. O, how dreadful, how terrible is it to be told by a man of his genius and knowledge, in so affectingly probable a manner, that true, real, happiness is ever unattainable in this world! – Thro' all the scenes, publick or private, domestick or solitary, that Nekaya or Rasselas pass, real felicity eludes their pursuit and mocks their solicitude. In high life, superiority, envy and haughtiness baffle the power of preferment, favour and greatness – and, with or without them, all is animosity, suspicion, apprehension, and misery! – in private families, disagreement jealousy and partiality, destroy all domestick felicities and all social cheerfulness, and all is peevishness, contradiction, ill-will, and wretchedness! And in solitude, imagination paints the world in a new light, every bliss which was wanting when in it, appears easily attained when away from it,

[4] hobby

but the loneliness of retirement seems unsocial, dreary, savouring of misanthropy and melancholy – and all is anxiety, doubt, fear and anguish! In this manner does Mr Johnson proceed in his melancholy conviction of the impossibility of all human enjoyments and the impossibility of all earthly happiness.

Saturday, July —

And so I suppose you are staring at the torn paper and unconnected sentence – I don't much wonder – I'll tell you what happen'd. Last Monday I was in the little parlour, which room my papa generally dresses in – and writing a letter to my grandmama. You must know I always have the last sheet of my Journal in my pocket, and when I have wrote it half full I join it to the rest, and take another sheet – and so on. Now I happen'd unluckily to take the last sheet out of my pocket with my letter – and laid it on the piano forte, and there, negligent fool! – I left it . . . Well, as ill fortune would have it, papa went into the room – took my poor Journal – read, and pocketted it. Mama came up to me and told me of it. O Dear! I was in a sad distress – I could not for the life of me ask for it – and so *dawdled* and fretted the time away till Tuesday evening. Then, gathering courage 'Pray papa', I said, 'have you got – any *papers* of mine?'

'Papers of yours?' said he – 'how should *I* come by papers of yours?'

'I'm sure – I dont know – but' –

'Why do you leave your papers about the house?' asked he, gravely.

I could not say another word – he went on playing on the piano forte. Well, to be sure, thought I, these same dear Journals are most shocking plaguing things – I've a good mind to resolve never to write a word more.

However, I stayed still in the room, walking, and looking wistfully at him for about an hour and half. At last, he rose to dress[5] – Again I look'd wistfully at him – He laughed – 'What, Fanny,' said he, kindly, 'are you in sad distress?' I half laugh'd. 'Well, – I'll give it you, now I see you are in such distress – but take care, my dear, of leaving your writings about the house again – suppose any body else had found it – I declare I was going to read it loud – Here, take it – but if ever I find any more of your Journals, I vow I'll stick them up in the market place.' And then he kiss'd me *so* kindly – never was parent so *properly, so well*-judgedly affectionate! I was so frightened that I have not had the heart to write since, till now, I should not but that – in short, but that I cannot help it! As to the *paper*, I destroy'd it the moment I got it . . .

We have had several little parties of pleasure since I wrote last, but they are not worth mentioning. My papa went on Thursday to Massingham, to Mr Bewly's . . .

I have been having a long conversation with Miss Young on journals. She has very seriously and earnestly advised me to give mine up – heigho-ho! Do you think I can bring myself to oblige her? What she says has great weight with me; but, indeed, I should be very loath to *quite* give my poor friend up. She says that it is the most dangerous employment young persons can have – that it makes them often record things which ought *not* to be recorded, but instantly forgot. I told her, that as *my* Journal was *solely* for my own perusal, nobody could in justice, or even in sense, be angry or displeased at my writing any thing.

'But how can you answer,' said she, 'that it *is* only for your own perusal? That very circumstance of your

[5] to change for dinner

22

papa's finding it, shows you are not so very careful as is necessary for such a work. And if you drop it, and any improper person finds it, you know not the uneasiness it may cost you.'

'Well but, dear ma'am, this is an "if" that may not happen once in a century.'

'I beg your pardon; I know not how often it may happen; and even *once* might prove enough to give you more pain than you are aware of.'

'Why, dear ma'am, papa never prohibited my writing, and he knows that I *do* write, and *what* I do write.'

'I question that. However, 'tis impossible for you to answer for the curiosity of others. And suppose any body finds a part in which they are extremely censured.'

'Why then, they must take it for their pains. It was not wrote for *them*, but *me*, and I cannot see any harm in writing to *myself*.'

'It was very well whilst there were only your sisters with you to do any thing of this kind; but, depend upon it, when your connections are enlarged, your family increased, your acquaintance multiplied, young and old *so* apt to be curious – depend upon it, Fanny, 'tis the most dangerous employment you can have. Suppose now, for example, your favourite wish were granted, and you were *to fall in love*, and then the object of your passion were to get sight of some part which related to himself?'

'Why then, Miss Young, I must take a little trip to Rosamond's Pond.'[6]

'Why, ay, I doubt it would be all you would have left.'

'Dear Miss Young! – But I'm sure, by your earnest-

[6] pond in St James's Park, London; it was later filled in, perhaps because unhappy lovers drowned themselves in it

ness, that you think worse of my poor Journal than it deserves.'

'I know very well the nature of these things. I know that in journals, thoughts, actions, looks, conversations – *all* go down; do they not?'

The conclusion of our debate was, that if I would show her some part of what I had wrote she should be a better judge, and would then give me her best advice whether to proceed or not. I believe I shall accept her condition; though I own I shall show it with shame and fear, for such nonsense is *so* unworthy her perusal.

I'm sure, besides, I know not what part to choose. Shall I take at random?

Wednesday, 10 August

Well, my Nobody I *have* read part of my Journal to Miss Young and what's more, let her choose the day herself, which was our Journey,[7] the day in which I have mention'd our arrival, &c. I assure you I quite triumph! prejudic'd as she was, she is pleas'd to give it her sanction, – *if it is equally harmless every where* – nay, says she even approves of it...

For some time past, I have taken a walk in the fields near Lynn of about an hour every morning before breakfast – I have never yet got out before six, and never after seven. The fields are, in my eyes, particularly charming at that time in the morning – the sun is warm and not sultry – and there is scarce a soul to be seen. Near the capital I should not dare indulge myself in this delightful manner, for fear of robbers – but here, every body is known, and one has nothing to apprehend.

[7] to King's Lynn

The Day-to-Day Life of a Parson

The Reverend James Woodforde

The Reverend James Woodforde (1740–1803) was born in Somerset. He attended Oxford University and was a curate in Somerset. After a period as subwarden at New College, Woodforde took up his duties as rector of Weston Longville in Norfolk on 24 May 1776. Entries from Woodforde's diary, known as *The Diary of a Country Parson*, are characteristically brief. They record fascinating minutiae of day-to-day happenings, such as his domestic arrangements, seaside breaks and a few personal blunders. Woodforde was rector of Weston Longville until his death.

26 October 1768

I had a poor little cat, that had one of her ribs broke and that laid across her belly, and we could not tell what it was, and she was in great pain. I therefore with a small pen knife this morning, opened one side of her and took it out, and performed the operation very well, and afterwards sewed it up and put Friars Balsam to it, and she was much better after, the incision was half an inch. It grieved me much to see the poor creature in such pain before, and therefore made me undertake the above, which I hope will preserve the life of the poor creature.

14 January 1774

Had a new wigg brought home this morning, which I put on before I went to dinner, it is a more fashionable one than my old ones are, a one curled wigg with two curls of the sides. I like it, and it was liked by most people at dinner. I gave the barber's man, Jonathan 0.1.0.[1] At back-gammon this evening with Milton only one gammon, and I lost to him by bad luck 0.10.6. I supped in the Chequer[2] and went to bed soon after.

3 June 1776

I breakfasted, dined, supped and slept again at Weston. My nephew breakfasted, dined, supped and slept at Weston. Two servant maids came to me this morning and offered their services to me. I agreed with them both and they are to come to me here Midsummer day next. One of them is to be an upper servant and she lived very lately with Mr Howes. A very pretty woman she is and understands cookery and working at her needle well. I am to give her per annum and tea twice a day – 5.5.0. She was well recommended to me by Mrs Howes and the reason she was turned away from Mrs Howes's was her not getting up early enough, as Mrs Howes told me. The other maid was recommended to me by Mrs Howes, she is a tenant's daughter of Mr Howes's, she is wooled.[3] I agreed to give her per annum – 3.10.0. She is to come at Midsummer also. She is to milk, etc.

Very bad all day in the toothache. The tooth is faulty. Mr Hardy and his Boy Mason at work for me all day.

[1] one shilling
[2] an inn at Oxford
[3] probably 'rustic'

Gave a man this morning for bringing home our dog 0.1.0. Dunnell the carpenter at work for me all day.

4 June

I breakfasted, dined, supped and slept again at Weston. My tooth pained me all night, got up a little after 5 this morning, & sent for one Reeves a man who draws teeth in this parish, and about 7 he came and drew my tooth, but shockingly bad indeed, he broke away a great piece of my gum and broke one of the fangs of the tooth, it gave me exquisite pain all the day after, and my face was swelled prodigiously in the evening and much pain. Very bad and in much pain the whole day long. Gave the old man that drew it however 0.2.6. He is too old, I think, to draw teeth, can't see very well.

5 June

I breakfasted, dined, supped and slept again at Weston. Very much disturbed in the night by our dog which was kept within doors tonight, was obliged to get out of bed naked twice or thrice to make him quiet, had him into my room, and there he emptied himself all over the room. Was obliged then to order him to be turned out which Bill did. My face much swelled but rather easier than yesterday tho' now very tender and painful, kept in today mostly. Paid and gave Will my servant this evening 0.5.0. Paid Mr Dunnell this evening part of a bill due to him from me, for 2 cows, 3 piggs, 3 pr. shoes, flower, tea, sugar, news papers, pipes, candles, pan, tobacco, beer, mustard, salt, washing, halters, comb and brush, crabs, bread and porterage of £14.9.3. the sum of a bank note - of – £10.0.0.

17 September

I breakfasted at Weston and afterwards set off to Yarmouth. Bill breakfasted at Weston and he went with me ... We got to Yarmouth about 4 o'clock, and there we dined, supped and slept at the Wrestlers in Church Square kept by one Orton. A very good house. After we dined we took a walk on the quay and viewed the Dutch vessells, about 70 sail which came in last night, to go a-fishing soon for herrings. The Dutch are very droll fellows to look at, strange, heavy, bad dressed people with monstrous large trousers, and many with large wooden shoes. To turnpikes[4] today from Weston to Yarmouth pd 0.1.6. My nephew is highly pleased with the town of Yarmouth.

19 September

We breakfasted, dined, supped and slept again at Yarmouth. After breakfast we each took a Yarmouth coach and drove down upon the coast, and called again at the fort. Will walked down there, at the fort today pd. 0.2.0. It was very pleasant and delightful indeed. Nothing can beat what we saw today – immense sea room, shipps and boats passing and repassing – the wind being rather high, the waves like mountains coming into the shore. We rode close to the ocean, the waves sometimes coming into our carriages. We returned about 3 o'clock. We had some fine smelts, shoulder of mutton rosted and tarts. In the evening we took a walk on the quay, as fine a one as ever was seen. A great deal of company walking backward and forward. We got on board an English vessel, and were treated

---

[4] tollgates on a main road where one must pay to pass

with wine, gin, etc. The sailors behaved very civil indeed to us, had a difficult matter to make them take anything, but at last I did, and all the silver I had, being only 0.1.0. She was a collier and going soon back to Sunderland.

15 April 1778

We breakfasted, dined, supped and slept again at home. Brewed a vessell of strong beer today. My two large piggs, by drinking some beer grounds taking out of one of my barrels today, got so amazingly drunk by it, that they were not able to stand and appeared like dead things almost, and so remained all night from dinner time today. I never saw piggs so drunk in my life, I slit their ears for them without feeling.

16 April

We breakfasted, dined, supped and slept again at home. My 2 piggs are still unable to walk yet, but they are better than they were yesterday. They tumble about the yard and can by no means stand at all steady yet. In the afternoon my 2 piggs were tolerably sober.

Hebridean Hospitality

James Boswell

James Boswell (1740–95) was a Scot by birth. He studied law,
like his father, Lord Auchinleck. However, his heart was set on
fame through writing and Dr Johnson was only one of his
many literary friends. He began to keep his celebrated journal
at the age of eighteen and it was the source for much of his
other writings, including his famous biography, *The Life of
Samuel Johnson*. In this extract from Boswell's *Journal of a Tour
to the Hebrides*, we join Boswell and Dr Johnson after they have
spent several days in the north part of the Isle of Skye. They
prepare to move south towards Slate Sound. Boswell's purpose
in writing this particular journal was as much to celebrate the
words and character of Johnson as to record the events and
surroundings.

Saturday, 25 September 1773

It was resolved that we should set out, in order to return
to Slate, to be in readiness to take boat whenever there
should be a fair wind. Dr Johnson remained in his
chamber writing a letter, and it was long before we
could get him into motion. He did not come to breakfast, but had it sent to him. When he had finished his
letter, it was twelve o'clock, and we should have set out
at ten. When I went up to him, he said to me, 'Do you
remember a song which begins,

"Every island is a prison
  Strongly guarded by the sea;
Kings and princes, for that reason,
  Prisoners are, as well as we."'

I suppose he had been thinking of our confined situation. He would fain have gone in a boat from hence, instead of riding back to Slate. A scheme for it was proposed. He said, 'We'll not be driven tamely from it': but it proved impracticable.

We took leave of M'Leod and Talisker, from whom we parted with regret. Talisker, having been bred to physick,[1] had a tincture of scholarship in his conversation, which pleased Dr Johnson, and he had some very good books; and being a colonel in the Dutch service, he and his lady, in consequence of having lived abroad, had introduced the ease and politeness of the continent into this rude region.

Young Col was now our leader.[2] Mr M'Queen was to accompany us half a day more. We stopped at a little hut, where we saw an old woman grinding with the *quern*, the ancient Highland instrument, which it is said was used by the Romans, but which, being very slow in its operation, is almost entirely gone into disuse.

The walls of the cottages in Sky, instead of being one compacted mass of stones, are often formed by two exterior surfaces of stone, filled up with earth in the middle, which makes them very warm. The roof is generally bad. They are thatched, sometimes with straw, sometimes with heath,[3] sometimes with fern. The thatch is secured by ropes of straw, or of heath; and, to

[1] educated as a doctor
[2] guide
[3] heather

fix the ropes, there is a stone tied to the end of each. These stones hang round the bottom of the roof, and make it look like a lady's hair in papers; but I should think that, when there is wind, they would come down, and knock people on the head.

We dined at the inn at Sconser, where I had the pleasure to find a letter from my wife. Here we parted from our learned companion, Mr Donald M'Queen. Dr Johnson took leave of him very affectionately, saying, 'Dear sir, do not forget me!' We settled, that he should write an account of the Isle of Sky, which Dr Johnson promised to revise. He said, Mr M'Queen should tell all that he could; distinguishing what he himself knew, what was traditional, and what conjectural.

We sent our horses round a point of land, that we might shun some very bad road; and resolved to go forward by sea. It was seven o'clock when we got into our boat. We had many showers, and it soon grew pretty dark. Dr Johnson sat silent and patient. Once he said, as he looked on the black coast of Sky – black, as being composed of rocks seen in the dusk – 'This is very solemn.' Our boatmen were rude[4] singers, and seemed so like wild Indians, that a very little imagination was necessary to give one an impression of being upon an American river. We landed at Strolimus, from whence we got a guide to walk before us, for two miles, to Corrichatachin. Not being able to procure a horse for our baggage, I took one portmanteau before me, and Joseph another. We had but a single star to light us on our way. It was about eleven when we arrived. We were most hospitably received by the master and mistress, who were just going to bed, but, with unaffected ready

[4] rough, poor

kindness, made a good fire, and at twelve o'clock at night had supper on the table.

James Macdonald, of Knockow, Kingsburgh's brother, whom we had seen at Kingsburgh, was there. He shewed me a bond granted by the late Sir James Macdonald, to old Kingsburgh, the preamble of which does so much honour to the feelings of that much-lamented gentleman, that I thought it worth transcribing. It was as follows:

> I, Sir James Macdonald, of Macdonald, Baronet, now, after arriving at my perfect age, from the friendship I bear to Alexander Macdonald of Kingsburgh, and in return for the long and faithful services done and performed by him to my deceased father, and to myself during my minority, when he was one of my Tutors and Curators; being resolved, now that the said Alexander Macdonald is advanced in years, to contribute my endeavours for making his old age placid and comfortable,

therefore he grants him an annuity of fifty pounds sterling.

Dr Johnson went to bed soon. When one bowl of punch was finished, I rose, and was near the door, in my way up stairs to bed; but Corrichatachin[5] said, it was the first time Col had been in his house, and he should have his bowl; and would not I join in drinking it? The heartiness of my honest landlord, and the desire of doing social honour to our very obliging conductor, induced me to sit down again. Col's bowl was finished; and by that time we were well warmed. A third bowl was soon made, and that too was finished. We were cordial, and merry to a high degree; but of what passed I have

[5] the laird of the place

33

no recollection, with any accuracy. I remember calling Corrichatachin by the familiar appellation of Corri, which his friends do. A fourth bowl was made, by which time Col, and young M'Kinnon, Corrichatachin's son, slipped away to bed. I continued a little with Corri and Knockow; but at last I left them. It was near five in the morning when I got to bed.

Sunday, 26 September

I awaked at noon, with a severe head-ach. I was much vexed that I should have been guilty of such a riot, and afraid of a reproof from Dr Johnson. I thought it very inconsistent with that conduct which I ought to maintain, while the companion of the *Rambler*.[6] About one he came into my room, and accosted me, 'What, drunk yet?' His tone of voice was not that of severe upbraiding; so I was relieved a little. 'Sir,' said I, 'they kept me up.' He answered, 'No, you kept them up, you drunken dog.' This he said with good-humoured *English* pleasantry. Soon afterwards, Corrichatachin, Col, and other friends assembled round my bed. Corri had a brandy-bottle and glass with him, and insisted I should take a dram. 'Ay,' said Dr Johnson, 'fill him drunk again. Do it in the morning, that we may laugh at him all day. It is a poor thing for a fellow to get drunk at night, and sculk to bed, and let his friends have no sport.' Finding him thus jocular, I became quite easy; and when I offered to get up, he very good-naturedly said, 'You need be in no such hurry now.'* I took my host's advice, and drank some brandy, which I found an effectual cure for my head-ach. When I rose, I went into Dr Johnson's room, and taking up Mrs M'Kinnon's

[6] Dr Johnson wrote and edited a magazine called *The Rambler*

prayer-book, I opened it at the twentieth Sunday after Trinity, in the epistle for which I read, 'And be not drunk with wine, wherein there is excess.' Some would have taken this as a divine interposition. . . .

This was another day of wind and rain; but good cheer and good society helped to beguile the time. I felt myself comfortable enough in the afternoon. I then thought that my last night's riot was no more than such a social excess as may happen without much moral blame; and recollected that some physicians maintained, that a fever produced by it was, upon the whole, good for health: so different are our reflections on the same subject, at different periods; and such the excuses with which we palliate what we know to be wrong.

(Boswell's own footnote to the point asterisked opposite.)

*My ingenuously relating this occasional instance of intemperance has I find been made the subject both of serious criticism and ludicrous banter. With the banterers I shall not trouble myself, but I wonder that those who pretend to the appellation of serious criticks should not have had sagacity enough to perceive that here, as in every other part of the present work, my principal object was to delineate Dr Johnson's manners and character. In justice to him I would not omit an anecdote, which, though in some degree to my own disadvantage, exhibits in so strong a light the indulgence and good humour with which he could treat those excesses in his friends, of which he highly disapproved.

In some other instances, the critics have been equally wrong as to the true motive of my recording particulars, the objections to which I saw as clearly as they. But it would be an endless talk for an author to point out upon every occasion the precise object he has in view. Contenting himself with the approbation of readers of discernment and taste, he ought not to complain that some are found who cannot or will not understand him.

A Naturalist's Eye-View

Gilbert White

Gilbert White (1720–93) was born in Selborne, Hampshire and educated at Oriel College, Oxford, eventually becoming curate of his home parish. His letters to two naturalists, Thomas Pennant and Daines Barrington, were written over a period of twenty years and were collected together for publication in 1789 as *The Natural History and Antiquities of Selborne*. The three letters which follow show how minutely detailed Gilbert White's observations of the creatures around him were. The first two concern tortoises, the third goldfish. In his third letter he refers to the Swedish naturalist Linnaeus (1707–78) who founded the classification system for animals and plants which is the basis of the system used by naturalists today.

12 April 1772

Dear Sir,

While I was in Sussex last autumn my residence was at the village near Lewes, from whence I had formerly the pleasure of writing to you. On the first of November I remarked that the old tortoise, formerly mentioned, began first to dig the ground in order to the forming it's hybernaculum,[1] which it had fixed on just beside a great turf of hepaticas.[2] It scrapes out the ground with its fore-feet, and throws it up over its back with its hind;

[1] winter retreat
[2] liverwort plants

but the motion of its legs is ridiculously slow, little exceeding the hour-hand of a clock; and suitable to the composure of an animal said to be a whole month in performing one feat of copulation. Nothing can be more assiduous than this creature night and day in scooping the earth, and forcing its great body into the cavity; but, as the noons of that season proved unusually warm and sunny, it was continually interrupted, and called forth by the heat in the middle of the day; and though I continued there till the thirteenth of November, yet the work remained unfinished. Harsher weather, and frosty mornings, would have quickened its operations. No part of its behaviour ever struck me more than the extreme timidity it always expresses with regard to rain; for though it has a shell that would secure it against the wheel of a loaded cart, yet does it discover as much solicitude about rain as a lady dressed in all her best attire, shuffling away on the first sprinklings, and running its head up in a corner. If attended to, it becomes an excellent weather-glass; for as sure as it walks elate, and as it were on tiptoe, feeding with great earnestness in a morning, so sure will it rain before night. It is totally a diurnal animal, and never pretends to stir after it becomes dark. The tortoise, like other reptiles, has an arbitrary[3] stomach as well as lungs; and can refrain from eating as well as breathing for a great part of the year. When first awakened it eats nothing; nor again in the autumn before it retires: through the height of the summer it feeds voraciously, devouring all the food that comes in its way. I was much taken with its sagacity in discerning those that do it kind offices: for, as soon as the good old lady comes in sight who has waited on it for more than thirty years, it

[3] controllable

hobbles towards its benefactress with awkward alacrity; but remains inattentive to strangers. Thus not only '*the ox knoweth his owner, and the ass his master's crib,*'[4] but the most abject reptile and torpid of beings dis-tinguishes the hand that feeds it, and is touched with the feelings of gratitude.

I am, &c. &c.

P.S.   In about three days after I left Sussex the tortoise retired into the ground under the hepatica.

21 April 1780   *Selborne*

Dear Sir,

The old Sussex tortoise, that I have mentioned to you so often, is become my property. I dug it out of its winter dormitory in March last, when it was enough awakened to express its resentments by hissing; and, packing it in a box with earth, carried it eighty miles in post-chaises. The rattle and hurry of the journey so perfectly roused it that, when I turned it out on a border, it walked twice down to the bottom of my garden; however, in the evening, the weather being cold, it buried itself in the loose mould, and continues still concealed.

As it will be under my eye, I shall now have an oppor-tunity of enlarging my observations on its mode of life, and propensities; and perceive already that, towards the time of coming forth, it opens a breathing-place in the ground near its head, requiring, I conclude, a freer respiration as it becomes more alive. This creature not only goes under the earth from the middle of November to the middle of April, but sleeps great part

[4] Isaiah 1:3

of the summer; for it goes to bed in the longest days at four in the afternoon, and often does not stir in the morning till late. Besides, it retires to rest for every shower; and does not move at all in wet days.

When one reflects on the state of this strange being, it is a matter of wonder to find that Providence should bestow such a profusion of days, such a seeming waste of longevity, on a reptile that appears to relish it so little as to squander more than two-thirds of its existence in a joyless stupor, and be lost to all sensation for months together in the profoundest of slumbers.

While I was writing this letter, a moist and warm afternoon, with the thermometer at 50, brought forth troops of shell-snails; and, at the same juncture, the tortoise heaved up the mould and put out its head; and the next morning came forth, as it were raised from the dead; and walked about till four in the afternoon. This was a curious coincidence! a very amusing occurrence! to see such a similarity of feelings between the two *Φερεοικοι*![5] for so the Greeks called both the shell-snail and the tortoise.

Summer birds are, this cold and backward spring, unusually late: I have seen but one swallow yet. This conformity with the weather convinces me more and more that they sleep in the winter. . . .

September/October 1781

Dear Sir,

When I happen to visit a family where gold and silver fishes are kept in a glass bowl, I am always pleased with the occurrence, because it offers me an opportunity of observing the actions and propensities of those beings

---

[5] pronounced 'phereoikoi' – 'carrying one's house with one'

with whom we can be little acquainted in their natural state. Not long since I spent a fortnight at the house of a friend where there was such a vivary, to which I paid no small attention, taking every occasion to remark what passed within its narrow limits. It was here that I first observed the manner in which fishes die. As soon as the creature sickens, the head sinks lower and lower, and it stands as it were on its head; till, getting weaker, and losing all poise, the tail turns over, and at last it floats on the surface of the water with its belly uppermost. The reason why fishes, when dead, swim in that manner is very obvious; because, when the body is no longer balanced by the fins of the belly, the broad muscular back preponderates by its own gravity, and turns the belly uppermost, as lighter from its being a cavity, and because it contains the swimming-bladders, which contribute to render it buoyant. Some that delight in gold and silver fishes have adopted a notion that they need no aliment. True it is that they will subsist for a long time without any apparent food but what they can collect from pure water frequently changed; yet they must draw some support from animalcula,[6] and other nourishment supplied by the water, because, though they seem to eat nothing, yet the consequences of eating often drop from them. That they are best pleased with such jejune[7] diet may easily be confuted, since if you toss them crumbs they will seize them with great readiness, not to say greediness: however, bread should be given sparingly, lest, turning sour, it corrupt the water. They will also feed on the water-plant called *lemna* (duck's meat), and also on small fry.

When they want to move a little they gently protrude

[6] small animals, unseen by the naked eye
[7] meagre

themselves with their *pinnae pectorales*;[8] but it is with their strong muscular tails only that they and all fishes shoot along with such inconceivable rapidity. It has been said that the eyes of fishes are immoveable: but these apparently turn them forward or backward in their sockets as their occasions require. They take little notice of a lighted candle, though applied close to their heads, but flounce and seem much frightened by a sudden stroke of the hand against the support whereon the bowl is hung; especially when they have been motionless, and are perhaps asleep. As fishes have no eyelids it is not easy to discern when they are sleeping or not, because their eyes are always open.

Nothing can be more amusing than a glass bowl containing such fishes: the double refractions of the glass and water represent them, when moving, in a shifting and changeable variety of dimensions, shades, and colours; while the two mediums, assisted by the concavo-convex shape of the vessel, magnify and distort them vastly; not to mention that the introduction of another element and its inhabitants into our parlours engages the fancy in a very agreeable manner.

Gold and silver fishes, though originally natives of China and Japan, yet are become so well reconciled to our climate as to thrive and multiply very fast in our ponds and stews.[9] Linnaeus ranks this species of fish under the genus of *cyprinus*, or carp, and calls it *cyprinus auratus*.

Some people exhibit this sort of fish in a very fanciful way; for they cause a glass bowl to be blown with a large hollow space within, that does not communicate with it. In this cavity they put a bird occasionally; so that you

[8] pectoral fins
[9] fish tanks

may see a goldfinch or a linnet hopping as it were in the midst of the water, and the fishes swimming in a circle round it. The simple exhibition of the fishes is agreeable and pleasant; but in so complicated a way becomes whimsical and unnatural, and liable to the objection due to him,

'Qui variare cupit rem prodigialitèr unam.'[10]

I am, &c.

---

[10] a line from *On the Art of Poetry* by the Latin poet Horace, describing the fault of a poet 'who wants to vary a single subject in an unnatural way'

The Loss of an Eye

Horatio Nelson

Horatio Nelson (1758–1805) was still a captain at the time the letter in this book was written, but during the Revolutionary Wars between England and France he was raised to Rear-Admiral and made Knight of the Bath. In the course of his naval service he lost not only an eye, but also his right arm. Nelson would have been away from his wife for quite some time and so to break the news of a serious injury to her by letter is his only available course of action. His words and tone reflect the reality of his situation. (Leghorn is now known as Livorno, in Italy; the other places are in Corsica. Josiah was Nelson's step-son.)

18 August 1794   *Off Leghorn*

I left Calvi on the 15th, and hope never to be in it again. I was yesterday in St Fiorenzo, and today shall be safe moored, I expect, in Leghorn; since the ship has been commissioned, this will be the first resting time we have had.

As it is all past, I may now tell you, that on the 10th of July, a shot having hit our battery, the splinters and stones from it struck me with great violence in the face and breast. Although the blow was so severe as to occasion a great flow of blood from my head, yet I most fortunately escaped, having only my right eye nearly deprived of its sight; it was cut down, but is so far recovered as for me to be able to distinguish light from darkness. As to all the purposes of use, it is gone; however the blemish is nothing, not to be perceived, unless told. The pupil is nearly the size of the blue part, I don't know the name.

At Bastia I got a sharp cut in the back. You must not think that my hurts confined me; no, nothing but the loss of a limb would have kept me from my duty, and I believe my exertions conduced to preserve me in this general mortality. I am fearful that Mrs Moutray's son, who was on shore with us, will fall a sacrifice to the climate; he is a Lieutenant of the *Victory*, a very fine young man for whom I have a great regard; Lord Hood is quite distressed about him. Poor little Hoste is also extremely ill, and I have great fears about him. One hundred and fifty of my people are in their beds; of two thousand men I am the most healthy. Josiah is very well and a clever smart young man, for so I must call him; his sense demands it.

Yours, etc.,
HORATIO NELSON

Walks and Wedding Bells

Dorothy Wordsworth

Dorothy Wordsworth (1771–1855) was the poet William Wordsworth's only sister and his lifelong companion. She wrote a number of journals in her lifetime including one kept mainly from their home, Dove Cottage, in Grasmere, Cumberland. She wrote as much for her brother's delight as for her own. In these extracts from her journal Dorothy and her brother William set out on a whistle-stop touring holiday. After visiting friends in Yorkshire they take a short trip to France. Their return to Yorkshire is marked by a happy event.

Thursday, 15 July – Monday, 4 October 1802

On Thursday morning, at a little before seven, being the 15th July, we got into a post-chaise and went to Thirsk to breakfast. We were well treated, but when the landlady understood that we were going to *walk* off, and leave our luggage behind, she threw out some saucy words in our hearing. The day was very hot, and we rested often and long before we reached the foot of the Hambledon Hills, and while we were climbing them, still oftener. We had a sandwich in our pockets which we finished when we had climbed part of the hill, and we were almost overpowered with thirst, when I heard the trickling of a little stream of water. I was before William, and I stopped till he came up to me. We sate a long time by this water, and climbed the hill slowly. I was footsore, the sun shone hot, the little Scotch cattle panted and tossed fretfully about. The view was hazy, and we could see nothing from the top of the hill but an indistinct wide-spreading country, full of trees, but the buildings, towns, and houses were lost. We stopped to examine that curious stone, then walked along the flat common. It was now cooler, but I was still footsore and could not walk quick, so I left William sitting two or three times, and when he followed me he took[1] a sheep for me, and then me for a sheep. I rested opposite the Sign of the Sportsman and was questioned by the landlady. Arrived very hungry at Rivaux. Nothing to eat at the Millers, as we expected, but at an exquisitely neat farmhouse we got some boiled milk and bread; this strengthened us, and I went down to look at the ruins.[2] Thrushes were singing, cattle feeding among green-grown hillocks about the ruins. These hillocks were scattered over with *grovelets* of wild roses and other shrubs, and covered with wild flowers. I could have stayed in this solemn quiet spot till evening, without a thought of moving, but William was waiting for me, so in a quarter of an hour I went away. We walked upon Mr Duncombe's terrace and looked down upon the Abbey. It stands in a larger valley among a brotherhood of valleys, of different length and breadth, – all woody, and running up into the hills in all directions. We reached Helmsly just at dusk. We had a beautiful view of the castle from the top of the hill, slept at a very nice inn, and were well treated – bright bellows and floors as smooth as ice. On Friday morning, 16th July, we walked to Kirby. Met people coming to Helmsly fair. Were misdirected, and walked a mile out of our way – met a double horse at Kirby. A beautiful view above

[1] mistook
[2] of Rievaulx Abbey

Pickering – Sinnington village very beautiful. Met Mary and Sara seven miles from G. H.[3] Sheltered from the rain; beautiful glen, spoiled by the large house – sweet church and churchyard. Arrived at Gallow Hill at 7 o'clock.

July 16th, Friday Evening. The weather bad, almost all the time. Sara, Tom, and I rode up Bedale. Wm., Mary, Sara, and I went to Scarborough, and we walked in the Abbey pasture, and to Wykeham; and on Monday, the 26th, we went off with Mary in a post-chaise. We had an interesting ride over the Wolds, though it rained all the way. Single thorn bushes were scattered about on the turf, sheep-sheds here and there, and now and then a little hut. Swelling grounds, and sometimes a single tree or a clump of trees. Mary was very sick, and every time we stopped to open a gate she felt the motion in her whole body – indeed I was sick too, and perhaps the smooth gliding of the chaise over the turf made us worse. We passed through one or two little villages, embosomed in tall trees. After we had parted from Mary, there were gleams of sunshine, but with showers. We saw Beverley in a heavy rain, and yet were much pleased with the beauty of the town. Saw the Minster – a pretty, clean building, but injured very much with Grecian architecture. The country between Beverley and Hull very rich, but miserably flat – brick houses, windmills, houses again – dull and endless. Hull a frightful, dirty, *brick-housey*, tradesmanlike, rich, vulgar place; yet the river, though the shores are so low that they can hardly be seen, looked beautiful with the evening lights upon it, and boats moving about. We walked a long time, and returned to our dull day-room but quiet evening one, quiet and our own, to supper.

---

[3] Gallow Hill, the home of the Hutchinson family

July 27th, Tuesday. Market day. Streets dirty, very rainy, did not leave Hull till 4 o'clock, and left Barton at about six; rained all the way almost. A beautiful village at the foot of a hill with trees. A gentleman's house converted into a lady's boarding-school. We had a woman in bad health in the coach, and took in a lady and her daughter – supped at Lincoln, duck and peas, and cream cheese – paid 2/-. We left Lincoln on Wednesday morning, 28th July, at six o'clock. It rained heavily, and we could see nothing but the antientry of some of the buildings as we passed along. The night before, however, we had seen enough to make us regret this. The minster stands at the edge of a hill over-looking an immense plain. The country very flat as we went along – the day mended. We went to see the outside of the Minster while the passengers were dining at Peterborough; the West End very grand. The little girl, who was a great scholar and plainly her Mother's favourite, though she had a large family at home, had bought 'The Farmer's Boy'.[4] She said it was written by a man without education and was very wonderful.

On Thursday morning, 29th, we arrived in London. Wm. left me at the Inn. I went to bed, etc. etc. After various troubles and disasters, we left London on Saturday morning at $\frac{1}{2}$-past 5 or 6, the 31st of July. (I have forgot which.) We mounted the Dover Coach at Charing Cross. It was a beautiful morning. The city, St Paul's, with the river and a multitude of little boats, made a most beautiful sight as we crossed Westminster Bridge. The houses were not overhung by their cloud of smoke, and they were spread out endlessly, yet the sun shone so brightly, with such a fierce light, that there was

[4] a poem by Robert Bloomfield

even something like the purity of one of nature's own grand spectacles.

We rode on chearfully, now with the Paris diligence before us, now behind. We walked up the steep hills, a beautiful prospect everywhere, till we even reached Dover. At first the rich, populous, wide-spreading, woody country about London, then the River Thames, ships sailing, chalk cliffs, trees, little villages. Afterwards Canterbury, situated on a plain, rich and woody, but the City and Cathedral disappointed me. Hop grounds on each side of the road some miles from Canterbury, then we came to a common, the race ground, an elevated plain, villages among trees in the bed of a valley at our right, and, rising above this valley, green hills scattered over with wood, neat gentlemen's houses. One white house, almost hid with green trees, which we longed for, and the parson's house, as neat a place as could be, which would just have suited Coleridge. No doubt we might have found one for Tom Hutchinson and Sara, and a good farm too. We halted at a half-way house – fruit carts under the shade of trees, seats for guests, a tempting place to the weary traveller. Still, as we went along, the country was beautiful, hilly, with cottages lurking under the hills, and their little plots of hop ground like vineyards. It was a bad hop year. A woman on the top of the coach said to me, 'It is a sad thing for the poor people, for the hop-gathering is the women's harvest; there is employment about the hops both for women and children.'

We saw the castle of Dover, and the sea beyond, 4 or 5 miles before we reached D. We looked at it through a long vale, the castle being upon an eminence, as it seemed, at the end of this vale, which opened to the sea. The country now became less fertile, but near Dover it seemed more rich again. Many buildings stand on the flat fields, sheltered with tall trees. There is one old chapel that might have been there just in the same state in which it now is when this vale was as retired, and as little known to travellers as our own Cumberland mountain wilds 30 years ago. There was also a very old building on the other side of the road, which had a strange effect among the many new ones that are springing up everywhere. It seemed odd that it could have kept itself pure in its ancientry among so many upstarts. It was near dark when we reached Dover. We were told that the packet was about to sail, so we went down to the custom-house in half-an-hour – had our luggage examined, etc. etc., and then we drank tea with the Honourable Mr Knox and his tutor. We arrived at Calais at 4 o'clock on Sunday morning, the 1st of August. We stayed in the vessel till $\frac{1}{2}$-past 7, then William went for letters, at about $\frac{1}{2}$-past 8 or 9 we found out Annette and C. chez Madame Avril dans la Rue de la Tête d'or. We lodged opposite two ladies, in tolerably decent-sized rooms, but badly furnished and with large store of bad smells and dirt in the yard, and all about. The weather was very hot. We walked by the seashore almost every evening with Annette and Caroline, or Wm. and I alone. I had a bad cold, and could not bathe at first, but William did. It was a pretty sight to see, as we walked upon the sands when the tide was low, perhaps a hundred people bathing about a quarter of a mile distant from us, and we had delightful walks after the heat of the day was passed away – seeing far off in the west the coast of England like a cloud crested with Dover Castle, which was but like the summit of the cloud – the evening star and the glory of the sky. The reflections in the water were more beautiful than the sky itself, purple waves brighter than precious stones, for ever melting away upon the sands. The fort, a wooden building, at the entrance of the harbour at Calais, when the evening twilight was coming on, and we could not see anything of the building but its shape, which was far more distinct than in perfect daylight, seemed to be reared upon pillars of ebony, between which pillars the sea was seen in the most beautiful colours that can be conceived. Nothing in romance was ever half so beautiful. Now came in view, as the evening star sank down, and the colours of the west faded away, the two lights of England, lighted up by Englishmen in our country, to warn vessels off rocks or sands. These we used to see from the pier, when we could see no other distant objects but the clouds, the sky, and the sea itself: All was dark behind. The town of Calais seemed deserted of the light of heaven, but there was always light and life and joy upon the sea. One night, though, I shall never forget – the day had been very hot, and William and I walked alone together upon the pier. The sea was gloomy, for there was a blackness over all the sky, except when it was overspread with lightning, which often revealed to us a distant vessel. Near us the waves roared and broke against the pier, and they were interfused with greenish fiery light. The more distant sea always black and gloomy. It was also beautiful, on the calm hot night, to see the little boats row out of harbour with wings of fire, and the sail boats with the fiery track which they cut as they went along, and which closed up after them with a hundred thousand sparkles, balls, shootings and streams of glow-worm light. Caroline was delighted.

On Sunday, the 29th of August, we left Calais at twelve o'clock in the morning, and landed at Dover at one on Monday the 30th. I was sick all the way. It was very pleasant to me, when we were in harbour at Dover, to breathe the fresh air, and to look up and see the stars among the ropes of the vessel. The next day was very hot. We both bathed, and sate upon the Dover Cliffs, and looked upon France with many a melancholy and tender thought. We could see the shores almost as plain as if it were but an English lake. We mounted the coach at $\frac{1}{2}$ past 4, and arrived in London at 6, the 30th August. It was misty, and we could see nothing. We stayed in London till Wednesday the 22nd of September, and arrived at Gallow Hill on Friday.

[Friday], September 24th. Mary first met us in the avenue. She looked so fat and well that we were made very happy by the sight of her; then came Sara, and last of all Joanna. Tom was forking corn, standing upon the corn cart. We dressed ourselves immediately and got tea – the garden looked gay with asters and sweet peas. Jack and George came on Friday evening, 1st October. On Saturday, 2nd, we rode to Hackness, William, Jack, George, and Sara single – I behind Tom. On Sunday 3rd, Mary and Sara were busy packing.

On Monday, 4th October 1802, my brother William was married to Mary Hutchinson.

Sense and Sensibilities

Jane Austen

Jane Austen (1775–1817) was born in Hampshire and is one of the most famous of all English novelists. From the age of twenty she kept up a close correspondence with her sister Cassandra and other members of her family and friends. She was always ready to offer her nephews and nieces advice when they asked, whether on the art of novel-writing or on matters of the heart. The two letters here are written to her niece Fanny Knight who has confided her feelings about a young man she has met to her aunt.

Friday, 18 November 1814   *Chawton, Hampshire*

I feel quite as doubtful as you could be my dearest Fanny, as to *when* my letter may be finished, for I can command very little quiet time at present, but yet I must begin, for I know you will be glad to hear as soon as possible, and I really am impatient myself – to be writing something on so very interesting a subject, though I have no hope of writing anything to the purpose. I shall do very little more I dare say than say over again, what you have said before.

I was certainly a good deal surprised at *first* – as I had no suspicion of any change in your feelings, and I have no scruple in saying that you cannot be in love. My dear Fanny, I am ready to laugh at the idea – and yet it is no laughing matter to have had you so mistaken as to your own feelings – and with all my heart I wish I had cautioned you on that point when first you spoke to me; but, tho' I did not think you then so *much* in love as you thought yourself, I did consider you as being attached in a degree – quite sufficiently for happiness, as I had no doubt it would increase with opportunity. And from the time of our being in London together, I thought you really very much in love. But you certainly are not at all – there is no concealing it.

What strange creatures we are! It seems as if your being secure of him (as you say yourself) had made you indifferent...

Poor dear Mr J. P.! Oh! dear Fanny! Your mistake has been one that thousands of women fall into. He was the *first* young man who attached himself to you. That was the charm, and most powerful it is. Among the multitudes however that make the same mistake with yourself, there can be few indeed who have so little reason to regret it; *his* character and *his* attachment leave you nothing to be ashamed of.

Upon the whole, what is to be done? You certainly *have* encouraged him to such a point as to make him feel almost secure of you – you have no inclination for any other person. His situation in life, family, friends, and above all his character – his uncommonly amiable mind, strict principles, just notions, good habits, *all* that you know so well how to value, *all* that really is of the first importance – everything of this nature pleads his cause most strongly. You have no doubt of his having superior abilities – he has proved it at the university – he is I dare say such a scholar as your agreeable, idle brothers would ill bear a comparison with.

Oh! my dear Fanny, the more I write about him, the warmer my feelings become, the more strongly I feel the sterling worth of such a young man and the desirableness of your growing in love with him again. I recommend this most thoroughly. There *are* such beings in the world perhaps, one in a thousand, as the creature you and I should think perfection where grace and spirit are united to worth, where the manners are equal to the heart and understanding, but such a person may not come in your way, or if he does, he may not be the eldest son of a man of fortune, the brother of your particular friend, and belonging to your own country...

Think of all this Fanny. Mr J. P. has advantages which do not often meet in one person. His only fault indeed seems modesty. If he were less modest, he would be more agreeable, speak louder, and look impudenter; and is not it a fine character of which modesty is the only defect? I have no doubt he will get more lively and more like yourselves as he is more with you; he will catch your ways if he belongs to you. And as to there being any objection from his *goodness*, from the danger of his becoming even evangelical, I cannot admit *that*. I am by no means convinced that we ought not all to be evangelicals, and am at least persuaded that they who are so from reason and feeling, must be happiest and safest. Do not be frightened from the connection by your brothers having most wit. Wisdom is better than wit, and in the long run will certainly have the laugh on her side; and don't be frightened by the idea of his acting more strictly up to the precepts of the New Testament than others.

And now, my dear Fanny, having written so much on one side of the question, I shall turn round and entreat you not to commit yourself farther, and not to think of accepting him unless you really do like him. Anything is to be preferred or endured rather than marrying without affection; and if his deficiencies of manner etc. etc. strike you more than all his good qualities, if you continue to think strongly of them, give him up at once . . .

We have heard nothing fresh from Anna.[1] I trust she is very comfortable in her new home. Her letters have been very sensible and satisfactory, with no *parade* of happiness, which I liked them the better for. I have often known young married women write in a way I did not like, in that respect.

You will be glad to hear that the first edit of M.P.[2] is all sold. Your Uncle Henry is rather wanting me to come to town, to settle about a 2d edit[3] . . . I am very greedy and want to make the most of it, but as you are much above caring about money I shall not plague you with any particulars. The pleasures of vanity are more within your comprehension, and you will enter into mine, at receiving the *praise* which every now and then comes to me, through some channel or other . . .

Yours very affecly.

J. AUSTEN

Your trying to excite your own feelings by a visit to his room amused me excessively – the dirty shaving rag was exquisite! Such a circumstance ought to be in print. Much too good to be lost.

Wednesday, 30 November 1814   *23 Hans Place, London*

I am very much obliged to you my dear Fanny for your letter, and I hope you will write again soon . . .

Now my dearest Fanny, I will begin a subject which comes in very naturally. You frighten me out of my wits by your reference. Your affection gives me the highest

[1] another of Jane Austen's nieces, who had recently been married
[2] edition of *Mansfield Park*
[3] second edition

pleasure, but indeed you must not let anything depend on my opinion. Your own feelings and none but your own, should determine such an important point. So far however as answering your question, I have no scruple. I am perfectly convinced that your present feelings, supposing you were to marry *now*, would be sufficient for his happiness; but when I think how very, very far it is from a *now*, and take everything that *may be* into consideration, I dare not say, 'Determine to accept him.' The risk is too great for *you*, unless your own sentiments prompt it.

You will think me perverse perhaps; in my last letter I was urging everything in his favour, and now I am inclining the other way; but I cannot help it; I am at present more impressed with the possible evil that may arise to *you* from engaging yourself to him – in word or mind – than with anything else. When I consider how few young men you have yet seen much of, how capable you are (yes, I do still think you *very* capable) of being really in love and how full of temptation the next 6 or 7 years of your life will probably be – (it is the very period of life for the *strongest* attachments to be formed) – I cannot wish you with your present very cool feelings to devote yourself in honour to him. It is very true that you never may attach another man, his equal altogether, but if that other man has the power of attaching you more, he will be in your eyes the most perfect.

I shall be glad if you *can* revive past feelings, and from your unbiased self resolve to go on as you have done, but this I do not expect, and without it I cannot wish you to be fettered. I should not be afraid of your *marrying* him; with all his worth, you would soon love him enough for the happiness of both; but I should dread the continuance of this sort of tacit engagement, with such an uncertainty as there is, of *when* it may be completed. Years may pass, before he is independent; you like him well enough to marry, but not well enough to wait. The unpleasantness of appearing fickle is certainly great – but if you think you want punishment for past illusions, there it is – and nothing can be compared to the misery of being bound *without* love, bound to one, and preferring another. *That* is a punishment which you do *not* deserve ...

I am to take the Miss Moores back on Saturday, and when I return I shall hope to find your pleasant, little, flowing scrawl on the table. It will be a relief to me after playing at ma'ams for tho' I like Miss H. M. as much as one can at my time of life after a day's acquaintance, it is uphill work to be talking to those whom one knows so little.

Only *one* comes back with me tomorrow, probably Miss Eliza, and I rather dread it. We shall not have two ideas in common. She is young, pretty, chattering, and thinking chiefly (I presume) of dress, company, and admiration ...

Thank you – but it is not settled yet whether I *do* hazard a 2d edition. We are to see Egerton today, when it will probably be determined. People are more ready to borrow and praise, than to buy – which I cannot wonder at; but tho' I like praise as well as anybody, I like what Edward calls *Pewter*[4] too. I cannot suppose we differ in our ideas of the Christian religion. You have given an excellent description of it. We only affix a different meaning to the word *evangelical.*

Yours most affectionately

J. AUSTEN

[4] slang for 'money'

How *The French Revolution* Was Mistaken for Wastepaper

Thomas Carlyle

Thomas Carlyle (1795–1881) was a historian born and educated in Scotland. He moved to London in 1834 with his young wife, Jane, and there completed his great work *The History of the French Revolution* in 1837. The letter here shows that this might never have been possible! The paper may have gone up in flames but fortunately the inspiration remained. Carlyle tells the story of the near disaster to his brother. ('Mill' was John Stuart Mill, the philosopher.)

23 March 1835   *5 Cheyne Row, Chelsea, London*

My dear Brother,

Your letter came in this morning (after sixteen days from Rome); and, tomorrow being post-day, I have shoved my writing-table into the corner, and sit (with my back to the fire and Jane, who is busy sewing at my old jupe of a dressing-gown), forthwith making answer. It was somewhat longed for; yet felt, in other respects, that it was better you had not written sooner; for I had a thing to dilate upon, of a most ravelled character, that was better to be knit up a little first. You shall hear. But do not be alarmed; for it is 'neither death nor men's lives' . . .

Mill had borrowed that first volume of my poor *French Revolution* (pieces of it more than *once*) that he might have it all before him, and write down some observations on it, which perhaps I might print as notes. I was busy meanwhile with Volume Second; toiling along . . . with the heart of a free Roman: indeed, I know not how it was, I had not felt so clear and independent, sure of myself and of my task for many long years.

Well, one night about three weeks ago, we sat at tea, and Mill's short rap was heard at the door: Jane rose to welcome him; but he stood there unresponsive, pale, the very picture of despair; said, half articulately gasping, that she must go down and speak to 'Mrs Taylor.' After some considerable additional gasping, I learned from Mill this fact: that my poor Manuscript, all except some four tattered leaves, was *annihilated*! He had left it out (too carelessly); it had been taken for wastepaper; and so five months of as tough labour as I could remember of, were as good as vanished, gone like a whiff of smoke.

There never in my life had come upon me any other *accident* of much moment; but this I could not but feel to be a sore one. The thing was *lost*, and perhaps worse; for I had not only forgotten all the structure of it, but the spirit it was written with was past; only the general impression seemed to remain, and the recollection that I was on the whole well satisfied with that, and could now hardly hope to equal it. Mill, whom I had to comfort and speak peace to, remained injudiciously enough till almost midnight, and my poor Dame and I had to sit talking of indifferent matters; and could not till then get our lament freely uttered. *She* was very good to me; and the thing did not beat us. I felt in general that I was as a little schoolboy, who had laboriously written out his *Copy* as he could, and was showing it not without satisfaction to the Master: but lo! the Master had suddenly torn it, saying: 'No, boy, thou must go and write it *better*.' What could I do but sorrowing go and try to obey.

That night was a hard one; something from time to time tying me tight as it were all round the region of the heart, and strange dreams haunting me; however, I was not without good thoughts too that came like healing life into me. Next morning accordingly I wrote to Fraser (who had *advertised* the book as 'preparing for publication') that it was all gone back; that he must not *speak of it* to any one (till it was made good again); finally that he must send me some *better paper,* and also a *Biographie Universelle,* for I was determined to risk ten pounds more upon it.

Poor Fraser was very assiduous; I got bookshelves put up (for the whole house was *flowing* with books) where the *Biographie* (not Fraser's, however, which was countermanded, but Mill's), with much else stands all ready, much readier than before: and so, having first finished out the Piece I was actually upon, I began *again* at the beginning. Early the day after tomorrow (after a hard and quite novel kind of battle) I count on having the First Chapter on paper a second time, no worse than it was, though considerably different. The bitterness of the business is past therefore; and you must conceive me toiling along in that new way for many weeks to come. This is my ravelled concern, dear Jack; which you see is in the way to knit itself up again – I have not been fortunate in my pen tonight: indeed for the last page I have been writing with the back of it. This and my speed will account for the confusion. Porridge has just come in. I will to bed without writing more. Good night, dear Brother.

Evcr yours!

A Blushing Bride

Queen Victoria

Queen Victoria (1819–1901) was Queen of Great Britain and Ireland, and Empress of India. She married Prince Albert of Saxe-Coburg-Gotha and worked closely with him as her consort and private secretary until his death. As the young Victoria describes the events of her wedding day and afterwards, it is clear that her feelings are those experienced by any bride, regardless of her station in life.

10 February 1840

The Ceremony was very imposing, and fine and simple, and I think *ought* to make an everlasting impression on every one who promises at the altar to *keep* what he or she promises. Dearest Albert repeated everything very distinctly. I felt so happy when the ring was put on, and by Albert. As soon as the Service was over, the procession returned as it came, with the exception that my beloved Albert led me out. The applause was very great, in the Colour Court as we came through; Lord Melbourne, good man, was very much affected during the Ceremony and at the applause. We all returned to the Throne-room, where the Signing of the Register took place; it was first signed by the Archbishop, then by Albert and me, and all the Royal Family, and by the Lord Chancellor, the Lord President, the Lord Privy Seal, the Duke of Norfolk (as Earl Marshal), the Archbishop of York, and Lord Melbourne. We then went into the Closet, and the Royal Family waited with me there till the ladies had got into their carriages. I gave all the Train-bearers as a brooch a small eagle of turquoise. I then returned to Buckingham Palace alone with Albert; they cheered us really most warmly and heartily; the crowd was immense; and the Hall at Buckingham Palace was full of people; they cheered us again and again. The great Drawing-room and Throne-room were full of people of rank, and numbers of children were there. Lord Melbourne and Lord Clarendon, who had arrived, stood at the door of the Throne-room as we came in. I went and sat on the sofa in my dressing-room with Albert; and we talked together there from 10 m. to 2 till 20 m. p. 2.[1] Then we went downstairs where all the Company was assembled and went into the dining-room – dearest Albert leading me in, and my Train being borne by 3 Pages, Cowell, little Wemyss, and dear little Byng. I sat between dearest Albert and the Duke of Sussex. My health and dearest Albert's were drunk. The Duke was very kind and civil. Albert and I drank a glass of wine with Lord Melbourne, who seemed much affected by the whole. I talked to all after the breakfast, and to Lord Melbourne, whose fine coat I praised. Little Mary behaved so well both at the Marriage and the breakfast. I went upstairs and undressed and put on a white silk gown trimmed with swansdown, and a bonnet with orange flowers. Albert went downstairs and undressed. At 20 m. to 4 Lord Melbourne came to me and stayed with me till 10 m. to 4. I shook hands with him and he kissed my hand. Talked of how well everything went off. 'Nothing could have gone off better,' he said, and of the people being in such good humour and having also

[1] m.= minutes; m. p.= minutes past

received him well; of my receiving the Addresses from the House of Lords and Commons; of his coming down to Windsor in time for dinner, begged him not to go to the party; he was a little tired; I would let him know when we arrived; pressed his hand once more, and he said, 'God Bless you, Ma'am,' most kindly, and with such a kind look. Dearest Albert came up and fetched me downstairs where we took leave of Mamma and drove off at near 4; I and Albert alone.

11 February

When day dawned (for we did not sleep much) and I beheld that beautiful angelic face by my side, it was more than I can express! He does look so beautiful in his shirt only, with his beautiful throat seen. We got up at $\frac{1}{4}$ p. 8. When I had laced I went to dearest Albert's room, and we breakfasted together. He had a black velvet jacket on, without any neckcloth on, and looked more beautiful than it is possible for me to say... At 12 I walked out with my precious Angel, all alone – so delightful, on the Terrace and new Walk, arm in arm! Eos our only companion. We talked a great deal together. We came home at one, and had luncheon soon after. Poor dear Albert felt sick and uncomfortable, and lay down in my room... He looked so dear, lying there and dozing.

12 February

Already the 2nd day since our marriage; his love and gentleness is beyond everything, and to kiss that dear soft cheek, to press my lips to his, is heavenly bliss. I feel a purer more unearthly feel than I ever did. Oh! was ever woman so blessed as I am.

Reviews and Sad Tidings

Charlotte Brontë

Charlotte Brontë (1816–55) and her sisters, Emily and Anne, were brought up in Haworth, Yorkshire, the daughters of a clergyman. All three wrote novels, of which Charlotte's most famous is *Jane Eyre*. The Brontë sisters' poems and novels were first published under the pen names of Currer, Acton and Ellis Bell. At first many reviewers found the books scandalous and unsuitable for women to read. In the first letter, Charlotte enjoys the joke of the secret behind their authorship in a letter to her publisher, although Emily is ill. The second letter is more sombre as the news of Emily's death is conveyed to her good friend Ellen Nussey.

22 November 1848

My dear Sir,

I put your most friendly letter into Emily's hands as soon as I had myself perused it. The *North American Review* is worth reading; there is no mincing the matter here. What a bad set the Bells must be. What appalling books they write. Today, as Emily appeared a little easier, I thought the *Review* would amuse her, so I read it aloud to her and Anne.

As I sat between them at our quiet but now some-what melancholy fireside, I studied the two ferocious authors. Ellis, the 'man of uncommon talents, but dogged, brutal and morose,' sat leaning back in his easy chair drawing his impeded breath as best he could, and looking alas, piteously pale and wasted; but it is not his wont to laugh, but he smiled half-amused and half in scorn as he listened. Acton was sewing, no emotion ever stirs him to loquacity, so he only smiled too, dropping at the same time a single word of calm amazement to hear his character so darkly portrayed. I wonder what the reviewer would have thought of his own sagacity could he have beheld the pair as I did. Vainly, too, might he have looked round for the masculine partner in the firm of 'Bell & Co.' How I laugh in my sleeve when I read the solemn assertions that *Jane Eyre* was written in partnership, and that it 'bears the marks of more than one mind and one sex.'

The wise critics would certainly sink a degree in their own estimation if they knew that yours or Mr Smith's was the first masculine hand that touched the MS of *Jane Eyre*, and that till you or he read it, no masculine eye had scanned a line of its contents, no masculine ear heard a phrase from its pages. However, the view they take of the matter rather pleases me than otherwise. If they like, I am not unwilling they should think a dozen ladies and gentlemen aided at the compilation of the book. Strange patchwork it must seem to them – this chapter being penned by Mr, and that by Miss or Mrs Bell; that character or scene being delineated by the husband, that other by the wife. The gentleman, of course, doing the rough work, the lady getting up the finer parts. I admire the idea vastly.

I must abruptly bid you goodbye for the present.

Yours sincerely,
CURRER BELL

23 December 1848

My dear Ellen,

Emily suffers no more from pain or weakness now. She will never suffer more in this world. She is gone, after a hard, short conflict. She died on Tuesday, the very day I wrote to you. I thought it very possible she might be with us for weeks, and a few hours afterwards she was in eternity. Yes, there is no Emily in time or on earth now. Yesterday we put her poor, wasted, mortal frame quietly under the church pavement. We are very calm at present. Why should we be otherwise? The anguish of seeing her suffer is over; the spectacle of the pains of death is gone by; the funeral day is past. We feel she is at peace. No need now to tremble for the hard frost and the keen wind. Emily does not feel them. She died in a time of promise. We saw her taken from life in its prime. But it is God's will, and the place where she is gone is better than she has left.

All Rulers Should Be Women

Beatrice and Sidney Webb

Beatrice and Sidney Webb (1858–1943 and 1859–1947) were well-known political figures at the beginning of the twentieth century. They helped to found the London School of Economics and later, on their return from travelling to Japan, China and India, they founded the journal *The New Statesman*. Sidney became a cabinet member in the British Government in the 1920s. Their travels were a holiday from work, but the diary which contains contributions from them both reflects their Socialist concerns.

On their grand tour of the East, Beatrice and Sidney were welcomed by one of India's female rulers, the Begum (Muslim princess) of the State of Bhopal, in central India. Beatrice spent the day discussing education and the role of women in society. These issues were as important to English politics of the time as to those of India. British women still had not been granted the right to vote in political elections; and the purdah system (named after a curtain, or screen), where women and men are kept apart, was still the norm in India.

17 February 1912   *Bhopal*

We have been two days in this State . . . on the invitation of the Begum, an exceptionally energetic and enlightened ruler. In the luxurious 'guesthouse' in which we were entertained we found an Anglican chaplain and his wife (Martin) who were touring round their extensive 'parish' of many hundred square miles, in which he dealt only with the few Anglican Christians. . . .

We have seen the jail, with a couple of hundred male and a dozen female prisoners, under the superintendence of the State Engineer, the son of a previous (Scotch) State Engineer... A large proportion (a quarter?) were under life sentences for murder, and there were only five belonging to a criminal tribe. (We infer from these facts that mere petty theft does not usually lead to jail.)

Under the guidance of the energetic lady doctor employed by the Begum (Mrs Dissent Barnes) we inspected her own hospital for women and children, and also the men's hospital (under Dr Sarabji, a parsee[1]). Syphilis is said to be almost universal, and unnatural vice as well; there is , in fact, no idea of sexual morality, among either Hindoos or Musselmans.[2] The most interesting feature was the attempt to regulate midwifery. The Begum had ordered the 'bais' or native midwives, who were to the last degree ignorant and superstitious, to attend classes held by the lady doctor; and the police were now stopping the practice, in Bhopal city, of any who had not received a diploma, or who, being qualified, had been suspended (by the lady doctor) for malpractice or carelessness. We have heard of no such attempt in British India. One thing we note about all these Central India States – Chhatarpur, Bhopal, Gwalior and the intervening British territory – is the very large proportion of land lying waste and unproductive. Vast stretches of sparse scrub and bushes, plains covered with a scanty natural herbage of

[1] person whose remote ancestors came from Persia
[2] Muslims

the coarsest kind, little bits of self-sown woodland of no pecuniary value, acre upon acre of boulder-strewn rock surface, weathering into brickmaking clay – all indicate that there is, here at any rate, no pressure of population on the soil. In Chhatarpur, for instance, the Dewan[3] was fully conscious of the need for more population, which would actually increase the yield per head. Wells and tanks – even more than irrigation canals – would apparently well repay their cost. The Begum of Bhopal is reported to be keenly alive to this need, but we did not learn what was being done. In Gwalior much is being spent on irrigation by the State.

We spent the afternoon with the Begum of Bhopal – at least we ladies did (the wife of the chaplain and two relations of officials and myself), Sidney and the other men being restricted to an hour's interview during which her Highness kept her veil down – just showing her eyes. The conversation was chiefly between the Begum and myself, as the other ladies were shy, and before the afternoon was ended, we were on very friendly terms.

The Begum of Bhopal is the one woman among the native rulers of India, and she is the third or fourth(?) woman in succession in the State of Bhopal (the eldest child, whether boy or girl, inheriting the Chieftain-ship). She is now an elderly woman with two grown-up sons and another at school. She has a great reputation as perhaps the most dutiful and statesmanlike of the Indian Chiefs. And certainly her personality fully bears out her reputation. She is small and thick in stature, but when she threw back her veil, on the departure of the men, I was surprised and attracted by the strong fine features and humorous and kindly expression

[3] State prime minister or minister of finance

(somewhat like the portrait of George Eliot) and with the total absence of any self-consciousness either as a woman or as semi-royalty. A wise old mother and an able business woman – not a bit of the great lady – clad in austerely simple garments, far more simple than those of the Mahommedan dames we afterwards met at her Purdah club, she is obviously a masterful woman, who is her own Prime Minister, having direct relations with each head of department. Her officials are devoted to her, but they record that she checks every penny of expenditure and insists perhaps overmuch in getting full value for her money. We talked about women, their position and their education, about the education of Chief's sons, about the sphere of religion, about Turkey and Egypt and their reform movements, about European society. She has recently been on a tour beginning with the coronation in England, and ending with her reception in Constantinople by the Sultan. She seemed to take the British Dominion for granted and to have an almost naïve respect for the King Emperor and the British Raj. But she did not wish the Indians or the followers of Islam 'Europeanised'. 'The English are very "habile"[4] – Europeans know a great deal – when they are evil they are powerful for evil. If our young men go there, when they are young they may get into bad hands, they may learn to abuse India and their own religion. I go to a house of a duchess in England and see all the magnificence and though I am an old woman, when I come back here, I think my own palace very plain and I am tempted to abuse it.'

And certainly when one followed her eyes round the homely and almost bare room – more like the parlour of a very large farmhouse – one saw what she meant. So

[4] an obsolete word meaning suitable or competent

she was against Chiefs' sons being sent to England: she was dissatisfied with the Chiefs Colleges as too luxurious and not sufficiently advanced in learning – she wanted her sons to go to an Indian public school where they would have to compete with boys who were going to be pleaders[5] and medical men and civil servants and engineers. 'I want my youngest son to go into business so that the race may become rich.' About religion and its relations to the state she was depressed. 'Our mulvis[6] are too conservative, they are against English education and science, our clever young men despise them and throw off religion – that is not good. The young Turks abuse religion; we shall not prosper unless we are true followers of our Prophet.' Apparently the old lady is a strong believer in Islam; what money she can spare from the temporal wants of her people she is lavishing on a new mosque which is to be more magnificent than any at Delhi. But at the same time she refused to give to beggars, and is a sworn critic of the idle mulvis. 'My mother used to give to beggars: I always send them away saying that "I pay teachers and doctors and nurses and not idle ones".' Her main preoccupation is the education of women. She wants the Mohammedan woman to become highly trained before she leaves off Purdah. She even approves of Purdah as a permanent institution – at any rate the modified Purdah of never going unveiled among men. 'The Turkish ladies are breaking Purdah, before they are fit for it. They are reading bad French novels and they do what is wrong.' So she has started a first-rate girls' High School – said to be one of the best in India – and she is trying to educate the married ladies by a Purdah club, where they have

[5] advocates or lawyers
[6] religious teachers

lecturers and talks once a week. As to the position that women should occupy, her views are somewhat conflicting. She is dead against the Suffrage Movement,[7] but she thinks that *all rulers should be women*. 'My mother and my grandmother were rulers before me; I lost my two daughters and now a son will succeed me. It is a great misfortune. Men care for their pleasures; they must have sport and races. A woman ruler is the mother of her people; her whole life is spent in thinking what is best for them.' And she seems to have been as good as her word. Not merely in education but also in public health she has been more advanced than the Government of British India. Three English lady doctors, and one Parsee medical man and an assistant, are engaged in hospital and dispensary work at Bhopal. At present they are trying to educate the native midwife, and the Begum has practically adopted the English Midwifes Act for Bhopal city. Any energy she has left over from the supervision of her Government she spends in translating English textbooks and school books. 'I want to start a department at Bhopal for translating and publishing good books for all India in the vernacular – I have tried to get a clever young man to come and live here and do that work, but I have not yet found one. What we want in India more than anything else are good books in Urdu and Hindi. You cannot teach children in a foreign language; they only pretend to understand what they read.'

She took us to the Purdah club held in one of the old palaces. Here were some twenty Mahomedan, and two Parsee ladies – the Hindus had not joined the club. With their bright-coloured and elaborately embroidered satin leggings and soft-silk gauze veils they made

[7] those who campaigned to secure votes for women

the dear old Begum with her cotton leggings and knitted woollen shawl look more than ever the Wise Old Woman, too wise and careful about the good of other people, to care how she looked herself. She was treated with great deference but with no kind of servility – more the deference shown to age and knowledge than that shown to social position. She chatted some half hour with them, and then, as the lecturer failed to come (a lady doctor who was to have lectured on 'First Aid' but who was detained by the dangerous illness of an infant), she rose and left, saying that she must go back and do her gardening. For the Begum has one or two relaxations – gardening, 'Sketching from Think' she calls it (i.e. driving out and seeing something and then trying to reproduce it), and playing on the piano with one finger, tunes she had heard played by the English teacher to her little grandsons. She has also adopted a handsome little granddaughter. I doubt not she would like to make her the Begum – for quite clearly she adores her. The little girl is extraordinarily handsome and intelligent looking – more like a North Italian than a typical Hindu. Her youngest son's wife – a girl of 13 – not yet allowed to live with her husband – was also under the care of the Begum and was being carefully educated.

Dulce et Decorum Est . . .

Michael Hewat

Michael Hewat (*d* 1915) was the brother of Sybil Hewat from whose memoirs his letters are taken. He was killed in action near Givenchy in France. Serving as a soldier in World War One he writes from France to his sister. Letters from the trenches were heavily censored and all references to places were obliterated. The letter of 9 March is the last one he sent from the Front. He was killed on the following day.

13 January 1915

We were near a village which had been badly shelled yesterday. I have never seen such a sight. Practically every house was utterly ruined – tremendous shell-holes in the road. I had a look at the church – a small one – no roof & very little wall standing – pieces of stained glass, images, broken pillars lying about everywhere, and the graveyard was all ploughed up... An officer there who had been right through this show said he had never seen anything like it.

Just after we left the Germans put some more shells into it, but I don't think they could have done more damage.

It is extraordinary how comfortable the men make themselves with no materials for doing so. Those in my lot boiled themselves several brews of tea, the only fuel being G.S. biscuit.

18 January

Had my first experience of decent shelling the day before yesterday, when we went up about a mile and a half behind the firing line on a fatigue.[1] Everybody was working away merrily when we heard the whistle of a shell coming. You could see everybody crouching down. It came down about 30 yards in front of us. It was so unexpected that everyone stood up and roared with laughter. However when they heard a second one coming they fairly ran for cover. None of our party was hit except R.E.'s[2] who were knocked down by large clods of earth which descended on them.

24 January

Trenches in a more or less collapsible condition. The first shell which burst 500 yards off knocked a large wet & heavy sandbag on my head, resulting in the loss of my second service cap, and a net gain of about a ton & a half of mud. Had bad weather there, first rain then hard frost, but worked it in twelve hour reliefs, so that had quite a good time. When not in trenches we were in a house just behind called Dead Cow House. The smell of it was the limit outside but curiously enough was alright when you got right in – not comfortable, but quite safe, as the smell though not shell & bullet proof was calculated to keep the King's enemies at a distance.

Very few casualties except through sickness owing to water in the trenches.

[1] a soldier's work other than actual fighting
[2] Royal Engineers

6 February

Now in a very famous part of the line.

Not a moment to write as I am left senior subaltern of the Corps. I am in charge at the moment. However I suppose I shall have to hand over when another Captain turns up. They may not be able to find one though. A lot of shells knocking round. We are quartered in a large red brick building of 3 storeys – rather an attractive mark for artillery. The Officers' quarters are in what was rather a nice private house. The Germans have bust open the safe, & left empty jewel cases scattered all over the place. A lovely piano – beautifully toned – also plenty of comfortable chairs. Everything just as they left it except for being bust about. Scrap books, family photos etc. all lying about. Plenty of crockery, which we use.

Have just had an order to proceed to another job – meant to write a decent letter – will manage to do so some day.

19 February

Billets.[3] Back here for forty-eight hours now; we do 48 in the trenches then 48 in reserve & so on ad infinitum. At present no one is allowed on leave as we are in a very important spot & everybody is frightfully scared that the Germans are going to try & break through here. I expect we shall have a long rest when we are finished here.

The billets are very nice. I get a bath whenever I come down here, & there is an armchair – a very rare thing in France.

---

[3] resting quarters

27 February

Your guess was more or less correct except that the place you mention is two miles inside the German lines. I couldn't face the vermi-something Dora[4] sent. The horrors of war aren't quite as bad as that stuff. Thank her for the chocolate and ginger. The Officers are beginning to get leave now. Two from this Battalion got 8 days' leave yesterday.

9 March   *Billets*

Dear Syb.

Thanks for your letter. The place you mentioned in your first letter was not the same as the one in your second!!! So I suppose you had forgotten which place you did mention. Nothing much doing here at present. We have been back for a day this time. We go up tomorrow and come back again, probably, in a couple of days, for some time. When next you are in Hereford could you get me a packet of 'Gillette' safety blades, half a dozen for 2p, which will last me for a long time. The photos are in a parcel ready to be sent back with the first person who goes on leave. You should not show them to too many people.[5] Please thank somebody very much for the magazines etc. Which arrived yesterday and we got them this morning when we came out of the trenches. Will write again soon – when we get back. Love to the Family.

Yrs.

MIGGS

P.S.   You might ask Dora to let me know what that tailor's bill was and I will send her a cheque for it.

[4] Michael's sister
[5] in case the regiment's position was recognised

Love in a Time of War

Vera Brittain

Vera Brittain (1893–1970) lived in Cheshire as a child and went to study at Oxford in 1914. The outbreak of war and the deaths of both her brother and her fiancé, Roland Leighton, caused her to break off her studies. She worked as a nurse until 1919, keeping a close record of her experiences, which were published as *Testament of Youth*. After the war she returned to Oxford and later became a freelance writer. In the first diary entry she is about to start her third term at Oxford. Roland is fighting in France. (Ypres in Belgium was the scene of a desperate battle between the British and Germans in April 1915.)

20 April 1915

I don't want to go back at all. Everything has changed so much since I was at college six weeks ago. On reading parts of my diary from the beginning of the year just now it struck me as curious how very little I said about Roland during last term, though he was in my mind so much. I think I loved him then, but it was nothing to what I do now. The development of my feelings towards him has been rapid & quite carried me away; it is almost terrible. When one loves deeply, it is almost impossible to remember what the time was like before one did. Yet I must go on trying to work – thinking that he may never read the letter I have so loved writing to him, or that the one I have received from him may be the last. I wrote him a long one today telling him much the same things as I have been writing just now. How I love writing to him!

21 April

Sometimes I can hardly believe I am I. I feel as if I were writing a novel about someone else, & not myself at all, so mighty are the things happening just now. If, that summer just after I came out[1] & things seemed as though they would always be stagnant & dull, someone had said to me 'Before three years are over you will not only have fallen deeply in love with someone, but that very person will be fighting on the battlefields of France in the greatest war ever known to man. And your anguish of anxiety on his account will be greater than anything you have dreamed possible,' I should not have believed it could really ever happen. Tonight – not only when I heard from Roland but before – I have been full of a queer excitement – almost exultation. There has been no apparent reason for it, so I very much wonder why.

Apparently the hill we have taken near Ypres is a real advantage to us, but our losses are reported to be heavy. That means terrible long casualty lists within the next few days.

26 December

Directly after breakfast I went down to Brighton, sent on my way with many good wishes from the others. I walked along the promenade, and looked at the grey sea tossing rough with white surf-crested waves, and felt

[1] was introduced into Society

a little anxiety at the kind of crossing he had had. But at any rate he should be safely in England by this time, though he probably has not been able to send me any message today owing to the difficulties of telephones and telegrams on Sunday and Christmas Day combined & the inaccessibility of Hassocks. So I only have to wait for the morrow with such patience as I can manage. Being a little tired with the energies of the night, I spent a good deal of the rest of the day in sleeping, thinking of the sweet anticipation of the morning and of the face and voice dearest of all to me on earth.

27 December

I had just finished dressing when a message came to say that there was a telephone message for me. I sprang up joyfully, thinking to hear in a moment the dear dreamed-of tones of the beloved voice.

But the telephone message was not from Roland but from Clare; it was not to say that Roland had arrived, but that instead had come this telegram, sent on to the Leightons by Mr Burgin, to whom for some time all correspondence sent to Lowestoft had been re-addressed:

T 233. Regret to inform you that Lieut. R. A. Leighton 7th Worcesters died of wounds December 23rd. Lord Kitchener sends his sympathy.

Colonel of Territorial Force, Records, Warwick.

31 December
New Year's Eve 11.55

This time last year He was seeing me off on Charing Cross Station after *David Copperfield* – and I had just begun to realise I loved Him. Today He is lying in the military cemetery at Louvencourt – because a week ago He was wounded in action, and had just 24 hours of consciousness more and then went 'to sleep in France'. And I, who in impatience felt a fortnight ago that I could not wait another minute to see Him, must wait till all Eternity. All has been given me, and all taken away again – in one year.

So I wonder where we shall be – what we shall all be doing – if we all still *shall* be – this time next year.

Longing for Home

Sir Ernest Shackleton

Ernest Shackleton (1874–1922) was an Irish-born explorer who travelled with Captain Scott on his first Antarctic expedition. Later he set a record himself, reaching a point just 97 miles from the South Pole. He died while on his fourth Antarctic expedition. Shackleton writes to his daughter in this letter. He was at the time attempting to mount a rescue mission for his men who were stranded on Elephant Island in the Scotia Sea, Antarctica. The rescue was eventually successful.

1 August 1916

My darling little Cecily,

Two years have gone by; child, since your old Daddy has seen you, and I am just longing to see my little girl again; though from your photo and from what Mummy tells me you have grown so much. It has been a long, long time to be away, and it has been a time full of work and danger, so that I want to come home and rest, and I want to walk with Mummy, you, Ray and Edward in Kensington Gardens again, and hear all you have been doing, and how you have been getting on at school, in fact, everything about you, darling.

This is a funny little ship I am on now; we all live in a small cabin, and the water comes down through the roof or rather deck, as the ship leaks, and all the time she rolls about. Just now I had to go up to alter the sails as a fair wind has come, and there is a chance that we may soon reach the Falkland Islands. We were not able to get through the ice to our men, and I have had to turn back, and now must wait for a bigger ship. I am very anxious about them, for they must have so little to eat now, unless they manage to get seals and penguins.

We are very short of water and have not been able to wash since we left South America three weeks ago; but that is nothing for I had no wash from October last year until 20th May this year, and had not my clothes off from the 1st August, 1915 till the 20th May, 1916.

I will have many stories to tell you of adventure in the ice when I return, but I cannot write them. I just hate writing letters, but I want you to get this and know I am thinking of you, my little daughter, and to tell you I loved your letter which you wrote last February to me. I know you will be a comfort and help to Mummy all the time I am away, and work well at school. Goodbye, darling, thousands of kisses,

From your loving Daddy

Lots of Love, Old Bean

P.G. Wodehouse

P.G. Wodehouse (1881–1975) worked for a bank before
becoming a writer. His most famous characters are Bertie
Wooster and his inscrutable valet, Jeeves. He wrote letters
almost every day and those here are to his adopted daughter,
Leonora. The first of Wodehouse's letters was written when
Leonora (Snorkles or Snorky) was at school. The second was
sent in response to the news that she was to be married to
Peter Cazalet, who ran a racing stables. Wodehouse signs off
with his family nickname, Plum. (Winks and Boo were the
family dogs.)

24 November 1920   *16 Walton St*
                                          London SW

Darling Snorkles,

We were so glad to get your letters and to hear that
you are having a good time. I thought you would like
Felixstowe. I'm so glad you've started riding.

The Haileybury match[1] was a disaster, darn it. We
were without Addison, and with him we should have
won easily, but still they had a couple of good men away.
Still we ought to have won anyhow, only the blighters
started the game scared, because Haileybury had
beaten Bedford so easily, and they let them score twice
in the first five minutes. It wasn't till after half time that

---

[1] a rugby match

we woke up, and then we simply put it all over them. But it was too late then, and we couldn't catch up. They scored four times and we scored three. We ought to have scored half a dozen times. Murtrie played a splendid game, and your little friend Mills, the fly-half, was brilliant at times, only he spoiled it by making one or two bad mistakes. He made one splendid run nearly the whole length of the field. On Saturday we finish up by playing Sherborne.

Great excitement last night. Mummie came into my room at half-past two and woke me out of the dreamless to say that mice had been snootering her. She said one had run across her bed. To soothe her I went to her room to spend the rest of the night, thinking that there may have been mice in the room but that she had simply imagined that they had got on the bed. We had hardly turned off the light when – zip! one ran right across the pillow!!! So then we hoofed it back to my room and tried to sleep there, but the bed was too small, so I gave up my room to Mummie and went back to the mice room. And for some reason or other Mister Mouse made no further demonstration, and I wasn't disturbed. But the result is that we are both very sleepy today. I have been trying to work, but can't rouse the old bean.

I am at present moulding the Archie stories into a book. The publisher very wisely says that short stories don't sell, so I am hacking the things about putting the first half of one story at the beginning of the book and putting the finish of it about a hundred pages later, and the result looks very good. For instance, I blend the Sausage Chappie Story and 'Paving the Way for Mabel' rather cunningly. You remember that the blow-out of the latter takes place in the grill-room. Well, directly it has happened there is a row at the other end of the grill-room, which is the Sausage Chappie having the finish of his story. Rather ingenious, what!

I went to Harrod's for the book-week, but didn't have to do anything except autograph a few books. [Herbert] Jenkins called up just now and wants me to come round and autograph a dozen of each of my books, as this book-week has caused a big run on them.

Mummie came out of the nursing home rather tired, as it was one of those places where they wake you up for breakfast at seven-thirty. She has been resting a lot since coming out, and seems much better now. We have got Ian Hay coming to dinner tonight.

The house is very still and quiet without our Snorky. We all miss you badly, especially Winifred. I have to go for walks by myself.

We listened to the Palladium on the electrophone[2] the night before last. The chap who sings 'Smith, Jones, Robins and Brown' had another good song, as a naval officer. Refrain as follows:

'It's wonderful the difference the Navy's made to me!
    Since first I went to sea,
I'm twice the man I used to be:
    They fixed me up with a uniform,
    And it's the uniform
    That takes the girls by storm.
I'm told that Beatty's simply crazy over me,
    And so he ought to be:
    For anyone can see
That, though I owe a lot to the Navy,
    It's nothing to what the Navy owes to me!'

---

[2] a variety programme from the London Palladium theatre, heard on an early type of radio

Droll, I think, yes, no? It sounds wonderful when I sing it. You must hear me some time.

Well, cheerio, old fright. Write again soon.

Your loving
PLUMMIE

6 November 1932   *Domaine de la Fréyère*
                                     Auribeau
                                     Alpes-Maritime

Darling Snorky,

You may well imagine (*peux bien figurer*) the excitement your letter caused in the home. Mummie was having a bath when she got it and rushed out with a towel round her shrieking for me. Winks barked, I shouted, and a scene of indescribable confusion eventuated.

It certainly was wonderful news. You know me on the subject of Peter. Thumbs up, old boy. Not only a sound egg but probably *the* only sound egg left in this beastly era of young Bloomsbury novelists... He really has got something. It is wonderful that you should be marrying a man who is not only the nicest chap I know but likes exactly the sort of life you like. You are bound to be happy.

And isn't it marvellous that you're so fond of Molly and such a friend of Thelma's, so that there's no awkwardness of taking on a strange family. I mean, if you are marrying – say, the Prince of Wales, there would be all that business of getting acquainted with the rest of them. Personally, I think any girl would be wise in marrying Peter simply to get Molly for a mother-in-law...

What fun you're going to have. You never could have been really happy with a London life. You need the country, and I can't imagine the country under more perfect conditions. Peter, apart from being Peter, has got such an interesting job. You'll love it. The only thorn in the whole thing is that we can't go yelling the news all over the place. I am so happy about it that I want to tell everyone I meet. I want to stop the French peasants on the road and say '*Figurez-vous, mon brave, ma fille est fiancée à M. Pierre Cazalet, le jeune homme le plus admirable de l'Angleterre.*'

Well, you will have gathered from all this that you have sold the idea to the old folks.

All my love, darling and tell Peter that he is just as lucky as you are, because there is no one like my Snorky.

PLUMMIE

P.S. Winks and Boo must be bridesmaids, carrying your train in their mouths.

In Hiding

Anne Frank

Anne Frank (1929–45) was a German Jew who fled to
Amsterdam with her family at the age of four. When the Nazis
occupied Holland the Franks went into hiding in an annexe
above offices and warehouses until they were betrayed in
August 1944. During that time the office workers (Koophuis,
Kraler, Henk, Elli, Miep and others) smuggled food, clothing
and other supplies to them, risking their own lives as they did
so. Anne and her sister Margot died in Belsen concentration
camp but her father survived and her diary (which she referred
to as 'Kitty' and which was discovered by accident in the
'Secret Annexe') was published in 1947.

When the entry begins, Anne's family, Mr Dussell, Peter Van
Daan and his parents have spent twenty-one months behind
the swinging bookcase which conceals the entrance to their
hiding place.

Tuesday, 11 April 1944

Dear Kitty,

My head throbs, I honestly don't know where to
begin.

On Friday (Good Friday) we played Monopoly,
Saturday afternoon too. These days passed quickly and
uneventfully. On Sunday afternoon, on my invitation,
Peter came to my room at half past four; at a quarter-
past five we went to the front attic, where we remained

until six o'clock. There was a beautiful Mozart concert on the radio from six o'clock until a quarter past seven. I enjoyed it all very much, but especially the *Kleine Nachtmusik*. I can hardly listen in the room because I'm always so inwardly stirred when I hear lovely music.

On Saturday evening Peter and I went to the front attic together and, in order to sit comfortably, we took with us a few divan cushions that we were able to lay our hands on. We seated ourselves on one packing case. Both the case and the cushions were very narrow, so we sat absolutely squashed together, leaning against other cases. Mouschi[1] kept us company too, so we weren't unchaperoned.

Suddenly, at a quarter to nine, Mr Van Daan whistled and asked if we had one of Dussel's cushions. We both jumped up and went downstairs with cushion, cat and Van Daan.

A lot of trouble arose out of this cushion, because Dussel was annoyed that we had one of his cushions, one that he used as a pillow. He was afraid that there might be fleas in it and made a great commotion about his beloved cushion! Peter and I put two hard brushes in his bed as a revenge. We had a good laugh over this little interlude!

Our fun didn't last long. At half past nine Peter knocked softly on the door and asked Daddy if he would just help him upstairs over a difficult English sentence. 'That's a blind,' I said to Margot, 'anyone could see through that one!' I was right. They were in the act of breaking into the warehouse. Daddy, Van Daan, Dussel and Peter were downstairs in a flash. Margot, Mummy, Mrs Van Daan and I stayed upstairs and waited.

[1] Peter's cat

Four frightened women just have to talk, so talk we did, until we heard a bang downstairs. After that all was quiet, the clock struck a quarter to ten. The colour had vanished from our faces, we were still quiet, although we were afraid. Where could the men be? What was that bang? Would they be fighting the burglars? Ten o'clock, footsteps on the stairs: Daddy, white and nervy, entered, followed by Mr Van Daan. 'Lights out, creep upstairs, we expect the police in the house!'

There was no time to be frightened: the lights went out, I quickly grabbed a jacket and we were upstairs. 'What has happened? Tell us quickly!' There was no one to tell us, the men having disappeared downstairs again. Only at ten past ten did they reappear; two kept watch at Peter's open window, the door to the landing was closed, the swinging bookcase shut. We hung a jersey round the night light, and after that they told us:

Peter had heard two loud bangs on the landing, ran downstairs and saw there was a large plank out of the left half of the door. He dashed upstairs, warned the 'Home Guard' of the family and the four of them proceeded downstairs. When they entered the warehouse, the burglars were in the act of enlarging the hole. Without further thought Van Daan shouted: 'Police!'

A few hurried steps outside, and the burglars had fled. In order to avoid the hole being noticed by the police, a plank was put against it, but a good hard kick from outside sent it flying to the ground. The men were perplexed at such impudence, and both Van Daan and Peter felt murder welling up within them; Van Daan beat on the ground with a chopper, and all was quiet again. Once more they wanted to put the plank in front of the hole. Interruption! A married couple outside shone a torch through the opening, lighting up the whole warehouse. 'Hell!' muttered one of the men, and now they switched over from their role of police to that of burglars. The four of them sneaked upstairs, Peter quickly opened the doors and windows of the kitchen and private office, flung the telephone on to the floor and finally the four of them landed behind the swinging bookcase – End of Part One.

The married couple with the torch would probably have warned the police: it was Sunday evening, Easter Sunday, no one at the office on Easter Monday, so none of us could budge until Tuesday morning. Think of it, waiting in such fear for two nights and a day! No one had anything to suggest, so we simply sat there in pitch darkness, because Mrs Van Daan in her fright had unintentionally turned the lamp right out; talked in whispers, and at every creak one heard 'Sh! sh!'

It turned half-past ten, eleven, but not a sound; Daddy and Van Daan joined us in turns. Then a quarter-past eleven, a bustle and noise downstairs. Everyone's breath was audible, otherwise no one moved. Footsteps in the house, in the private office, kitchen, then ... on our staircase. No one breathed audibly now, footsteps on our staircase, then a rattling of the swinging bookcase. This moment is indescribable. 'Now we are lost!' I said, and could see us all being taken away by the Gestapo that very night. Twice they rattled at the bookcase, then there was nothing, the footsteps withdrew, we were saved so far. A shiver seemed to pass from one to another, I heard someone's teeth chattering, no one said a word.

There was not another sound in the house, but a light was burning on our landing, right in front of the bookcase. Could that be because it was a secret bookcase? Perhaps the police had forgotten the light? Would someone come back to put it out? Tongues loosened, there was no one in the house any longer – but perhaps there was someone on guard outside.

Next we did three things: we went over again what we supposed had happened, we trembled with fear, and we had to go to the lavatory. The buckets were in the attic, so all we had was Peter's tin wastepaper basket. Van Daan went first, then Daddy, but Mummy was too shy to face it. Daddy brought the wastepaper basket into the room, where Margot, Mrs Van Daan and I gladly made use of it. Finally Mummy decided to do so too. People kept on asking for paper – fortunately I had some in my pocket!

The tin smelt ghastly, everything went on in a whisper, we were tired, it was twelve o'clock. 'Lie down on the floor then and sleep.' Margot and I were each given a pillow and one blanket; Margot lying just near the store-cupboard and I between the table legs. The smell wasn't quite so bad when one was on the floor, but still Mrs Van Daan quietly fetched some chlorine, a tea towel over the pot serving as a second expedient.

Talk, whispers, fear, stink, people breaking wind, and always someone on the pot: then try to go to sleep! However, by half-past two I was so tired that I knew no more until half-past three. I awoke when Mrs Van Daan laid her head on my foot.

'For Heaven's sake, give me something to put on!' I asked. I was given something, but don't ask what – a pair of woollen knickers over my pyjamas, a red jumper, and a black shirt, white over-socks and a pair of sports stockings full of holes. Then Mrs Van Daan sat in the chair and her husband came and lay on my feet. I lay thinking till half-past three, shivering the whole time, which prevented Van Daan from sleeping. I prepared myself for the return of the police, then we'd have to say that we were in hiding; they would either be good

Dutch people, then we'd be saved, or the N.S.B.,[2] then we'd have to bribe them!

'In that case, destroy the radio,' sighed Mrs Van Daan. 'Yes, in the stove!' replied her husband. 'If they find us, then let them find the radio as well!'

'Then they will find Anne's diary,' added Daddy. 'Burn it then,' suggested the most terrified member of the party. This, and when the police rattled the cupboard door, were my worst moments. 'Not my diary, if my diary goes, I go with it!' But luckily Daddy didn't answer.

There is no object in recounting all the conversations that I can still remember; so much was said. I comforted Mrs Van Daan, who was very scared. We talked about escaping and being questioned by the Gestapo, about ringing up, and being brave.

'We must behave like soldiers, Mrs Van Daan. If all is up now, then let's go for Queen and Country, for freedom, truth and right, as they always say on Radio Orange. The only thing that is really rotten is that we get a lot of other people into trouble too.'

Mr Van Daan changed places again with his wife after an hour, and Daddy came and sat beside me. The men smoked non-stop, now and then there was a deep sigh, then someone went on the pot and everything began all over again.

Four o'clock, five o'clock, half-past five. Then I went and sat with Peter by his window and listened, so close together that we could feel each other's bodies quivering; we spoke a word or two now and then, and listened attentively. In the room next door they took down the black-out. They wanted to ring up Koophuis at seven o'clock and get him to send someone round.

[2] Dutch Nazi party

Then they wrote down everything they wanted to tell Koophuis over the phone. The risk that the police on guard at the door, or in the warehouse, might hear the telephone was very great, but the danger of the police returning was even greater.

The points were these:

Burglars broken in: police have been in the house, as far as the swinging bookcase, but no further.

Burglars apparently disturbed, forced open the door in the warehouse and escaped through the garden.

Main entrance bolted, Kraler must have used the second door when he left. The typewriters and adding machine are safe in the black case in the private office.

Try to warn Henk and fetch the key from Elli, then go and look round the office – on the pretext of feeding the cat.

Everything went according to plan. Koophuis was rung up, the typewriters which we had upstairs were put in the case. Then we sat round the table again and waited for Henk or the police.

Peter had fallen asleep and Van Daan and I were lying on the floor, when we heard loud footsteps downstairs. I got up quietly: 'That's Henk.'

'No, no, it's the police,' some of the others said.

Someone knocked at the door, Miep whistled. This was too much for Mrs Van Daan, she turned as white as a sheet and sank limply into a chair; had the tension lasted one minute longer she would have fainted.

Our room was a perfect picture when Miep and Henk entered, the table alone would have been worth photographing! A copy of *Cinema and Theatre*, covered with jam and a remedy for diarrhoea, opened at a page of dancing girls, two jam pots, two partly eaten pieces of bread, a mirror, comb, matches, ash, cigarettes, tobacco, ash-tray, books, a pair of pants, a torch, toilet-paper, etc. etc., lay jumbled together in variegated splendour.

Of course Henk and Miep were greeted with shouts and tears. Henk mended the hole in the door with some planks and soon went off again to inform the police of the burglary. Miep had also found a letter under the warehouse door from the night watchman Slagter, who had noticed the hole and warned the police, whom he would also visit.

So we had half an hour to tidy ourselves. I've never seen such a change take place in half an hour. Margot and I took the bedclothes downstairs, went to the W.C., washed and did our teeth and hair. After that I tidied the room a bit and went upstairs again. The table there was already cleared, so we ran off some water and made coffee and tea, boiled the milk and laid the table for lunch. Daddy and Peter emptied the potties and cleaned them with warm water and chlorine.

At eleven o'clock we sat round the table with Henk, who was back by that time, and slowly things began to be more normal and cosy again. Henk's story was as follows:

Mr Slagter was asleep, but his wife told Henk that her husband had found the hole in our door when he was doing his tour round the canals, and that he had fetched a policeman, who had gone through the building with him. He would be coming to see Kraler on Tuesday and would tell him more then. At the police station they knew nothing of the burglary yet, but the policeman had made a note of it at once and would come and look round on Tuesday. On the way back Henk happened to meet our greengrocer at the corner, and told him that the house had been broken into. 'I know that,' he said quite coolly. 'I was passing last evening with my wife and saw the hole in the door. My wife wanted to walk on, but I just had a look in with my torch; then the thieves cleared at once. To be on the safe side, I didn't ring up the police, as with you I didn't think it was the thing to do. I don't know anything, but I guess a lot.'

Henk thanked him and went on. The man obviously guesses that we're here, because he always brings the potatoes during the lunch hour. Decent chap!

It was one by the time Henk had gone and we'd finished the washing-up. We all went for a sleep. I awoke at a quarter to three and saw that Mr Dussel had already disappeared. Quite by chance, and with my sleepy eyes, I ran to Peter in the bathroom; he had just come down. We arranged to meet downstairs.

I tidied myself and went down. 'Do you still dare to go to the front attic?' he asked. I nodded, fetched my pillow and we went up to the attic. It was glorious weather, and soon the sirens were wailing; we stayed where we were. Peter put his arm round my shoulder, and I put mine round his and so we remained, our arms round each other, quietly waiting until Margot came to fetch us for coffee at four o'clock.

We finished our bread, drank lemonade and joked (we were able to again), and everything else went normally. In the evening I thanked Peter because he was the bravest of us all.

None of us has ever been in such danger as that night. God truly protected us; just think of it – the police at our secret cupboard, the light on right in front of it, and still we remained undiscovered.

If the invasion comes, and bombs with it, then it is each man for himself, but in this case the fear was also for our good, innocent protectors. 'We are saved, go on saving us!' That is all we can say.

This affair has brought quite a number of changes with it. Mr Dussel no longer sits downstairs in Kraler's office in the evenings, but in the bathroom instead. Peter goes round the house for a check-up at half-past eight and half-past nine. Peter isn't allowed to have his window open at nights any more. No one is allowed to pull the plug after half-past nine. This evening there's a carpenter coming to make the warehouse doors even stronger.

Now there are debates going on all the time in the 'Secret Annexe.' Kraler reproached us for our carelessness. Henk, too, said that in a case like that we must never go downstairs. We have been pointedly reminded that we are in hiding, that we are Jews in chains, chained to one spot, without any rights but with a thousand duties. We Jews mustn't show our feelings, must be brave and strong, must accept all inconveniences and not grumble, must do what is within our power and trust in God. Some time this terrible war will be over. Surely the time will come when we are people again, and not just Jews.

Who has inflicted this upon us? Who has made us Jews different to all other people? Who has allowed us to suffer so terribly up till now? It is God that has made us as we are, but it will be God, too, who will raise us up again. If we bear all this suffering and if there are still Jews left, when it is over, then Jews, instead of being doomed, will be held up as an example. Who knows, it might even be our religion from which the world and all peoples learn good, and for that reason and that reason only do we have to suffer now. We can never become just Netherlanders, or just English, or representatives of any country for that matter, we will always remain Jews, but we want to, too.

Be brave! Let us remain aware of our task and not

grumble, a solution will come, God has never deserted our people. Right through the ages there have been Jews, through all the ages they have had to suffer, but it has made them strong too; the weak fall, but the strong will remain and never go under!

During that night I really felt that I had to die, I waited for the police, I was prepared, as the soldier is on the battlefield. I was eager to lay down my life for the country, but now, now I've been saved again, now my first wish after the war is that I may become Dutch! I love the Dutch, I love this country, I love the language and want to work here. And even if I have to write to the Queen myself, I will not give up until I have reached my goal.

I am becoming still more independent of my parents, young as I am, I face life with more courage than Mummy; my feeling for justice is immovable, and truer than hers. I know what I want, I have a goal, an opinion, I have a religion and love. Let me be myself and then I am satisfied. I know that I'm a woman, a woman with inward strength and plenty of courage.

If God lets me live, I shall attain more than Mummy ever has done, I shall not remain insignificant, I shall work in the world and for mankind!

And now I know that first and foremost I shall require courage and cheerfulness!

Yours,
ANNE

Keeping the Homefires Burning

Nella Last

Nella Last, a middle-aged housewife living in Barrow-in-Furness in Cumbria, kept a diary throughout the Second World War (1939–45). Her husband was a joiner and they had two sons. At 11.15 on the morning of Sunday, 3 September 1939, Neville Chamberlain, Britain's Prime Minister, announced on radio that Britain was at war. Nella Last and her family clustered around the wireless to hear the fateful news.

By 1941 food supplies to Britain had become scarce and the work of civilians, such as the Women's Volunteer Service, of which Nella was a member, had become important. There was intense bombing of British cities by the Germans and the shipyard at Barrow-in-Furness near her home was a prime target. On 6 August 1945, the allies used a new type of bomb for the first time. The US Air Force dropped an atomic bomb on Hiroshima in Japan, and another three days later on Nagasaki.

Sunday, 3 September 1939
Bedtime

Well, we know the worst. Whether it was a kind of incredulous stubbornness or a faith in my old astrological friend who was right in the last crisis when he said 'No war', I *never* thought it would come. Looking back I think it was akin to a belief in a fairy's wand which was going to be waved.

I'm a self-reliant kind of person, but today I've longed for a close woman friend – for the first time in my life. When I heard Mr Chamberlain's voice, so slow and solemn, I seemed to see Southsea Prom the July before the last crisis. The Fleet came into Portsmouth from Weymouth and there were hundreds of extra ratings[1] walking up and down. There was a sameness about them that was not due to their clothes alone, and it puzzled me. It was the look on their faces – a slightly brooding, faraway look. They all had it – even the jolly-looking boys – and I felt I wanted to rush up and ask them what they could see that I could not. And now I know.

The wind got up and brought rain, but on the Walney shore men and boys worked filling sand-bags. I could tell by the dazed look on many faces that I had not been alone in my belief that 'something' would turn up to prevent war. The boys brought a friend in and insisted on me joining in a game, but I could not keep it up. I've tried deep breathing, relaxing, knitting and more aspirins than I can remember, but all I can see are those boys with their look of 'beyond'.

My younger boy will go in just over a week. His friend who has no mother and is like another son will go soon – he is twenty-six. My elder boy works in Manchester. As a tax inspector he is at present in a 'reserved occupation'.

Easter Monday, 14 April 1941

Last night, a noise like the crack of Doom sounded, and brought us springing from our beds to rush downstairs, and my husband said crossly, 'It's only an explosion

[1] sailors

somewhere. If it had been a bomb, there would have been the sound of a plane – or the alert. I'm going back to bed!' Just then the alert sounded, and a plane flying so low that we feared for our housetop. Our gun fired one volley, then stopped; there was a frightful bang – crack – bang, the rattle of machine-guns and the sound of chaser planes. The noise was terrifying – all so near and low down.

Nothing more happened after the sound died away, as if the enemy was chased far out to sea, and after the all-clear we went to bed. This morning my husband was called out early and he worked hard all day, with all the men he could collect, to board up shop windows. There was only one stick of bombs, but the destruction from the two they *have* found is unbelievable. One big commercial hotel got one, and a little street the other: the former and four houses of the latter are just piles of rubble, and no one was saved from them.

I could not have believed so few bombs could do so much damage. It made me sick to think what *two* airplanes and about four bombs could do to our town. After taking out the big ton and a half bomb dropped last week, the expert said that it could have laid all in ruins for two square miles; and I believe it now. Bulging walls, gaping windows, hundreds of broken panes of glass, crazily leaning chimneys, flying ambulances, dirty tired H.G.[2] wardens, ordinary citizens in demolition gangs working like men possessed, with their shovels and picks going like clockwork as if to the sound of a hidden shanty, dazed-looking men who were piling mattresses on hand-carts where people had been ordered to evacuate, crowds of quiet white-faced specta-tors who needed no 'Pass along' from the guarding

[2] Home Guard

police and H.G. – they wanted to see, but not to linger over the sight of destruction.

My husband came in tired and saddened by all the mess and destruction and we went for a short drive to the Coast Road, to fill the remainder of the sandbags I had made. I will go on making them from any strong bits of material I can piece together; they would do for others if we did not want them. My husband said, 'I think we will order an indoor shelter after all.'

We have ordered one by tonight's post, and will put it up in the lounge. I'll keep the rubber camp beds blown up ready in the shelter, and have rugs and blankets easy to get at. We have talked about it long enough – my husband doesn't like to make decisions of any kind, and if I make the pace too much, he takes the other road. It makes him stubborn, so I've to be very tactful. Today has shown him how quickly a house or building can be a heap of rubbish.

Tuesday, 15 April
Twelve o'clock

Sounds of bombs and waves of planes going over to either the Clyde or Northern Ireland, machine-gunning and our own guns – all making an inferno of sound, and the crump of bombs falling in the centre of the town is dreadful. I've knitted and written to the boys, and I feel I can never sleep again – as if my eyes were propped wide open. We sit by the dining-room fire in the lulls, and then scatter for the reinforced part under the stairs.

Two o'clock

I wonder if there will be anything left of the centre of

town, there are such dreadful crumps. My back feels as if my whole spine is burning hot, but I cannot relax and lie down, for every fifteen minutes or so we run for cover while shrapnel pours on to the roof, and bombs dropped somewhere make the doors and windows shake and rattle, as if someone is trying to force their way in. My husband said, 'I wish I had ordered the indoor shelter when you first mentioned it – we would have had it by now, and could have lain down in safety and comfort.'

Four o'clock

The devil planes must be coming back now – a hundred must have passed over tonight. I think I'd like to cry or swear or something. I've got a tight knot in my head. My husband is very nervy, though, and it would upset him if he knew how terrified I felt. I don't like knitting, but I've been glad to have something in my fingers. The powders that I got for the lads are no use, and I fell back on an aspirin for old Sol and half a one in milk for poor little Mr Murphy. Sol paced the hearthrug and swayed from side to side like a lion – I did not know my old dog. They are such odd, sensible animals. They took their aspirins as if they knew it was for their good, and then lay down where I pointed, in the 'well' of the strong, oak gateleg table, and were no more trouble.

Wednesday, 16 April

The all-clear went at four o'clock and we gladly crawled to bed, only to be wakened by the first of several frantic shopkeepers at 5.30. Four more came before my husband could get a little breakfast and go, and I lost count of them before dinner-time. It's the centre of town again – a church, printing office and public baths gone, and such a lot of houses and shops uninhabitable, with cinemas roped off and no shops opened. I felt glad I'd thought to leave my order at the grocer's, for he was in his shop and got up any orders and sent them out. It was such a good order – a tin of unsweetened milk and one of pears, all my rations – even a quarter of cheese and a whole pound of lovely little biscuits (half a pound for me and half a pound for my tea box at the Centre). I do feel so worried about our stores and workroom – no one is allowed in the 'danger zone' yet.

Ruth came, looking tired out, and I said, 'Today, Ruth, do only what is absolutely necessary, for I'm not going to work with you at all.' I filled with water every clean bottle that I had, changed all the water in my buckets and brought Cliff's two good suits down to the clothes closet under the reinforced under-stairs – also his dinner-suit – and packed his good ties and handkerchiefs in the pockets of the jackets. I packed my good costume and my husband's best suit into a strong cardboard box, and tied it with strong string. In another box, I put a new coat piece and dress piece that I had treasured since just after the outbreak of war. All my best satin and crêpe-de-chine undies – there will be no more remnants of lovely oddments in the market – my three pairs of silk stockings that are for high days and holidays, my nearly new shoes, my lovely Chinese embroidered handkerchiefs, a good pair of chamois gloves and some decent blouses. My hatbox, with my fur and plain black evening-dress and shoes, came down too. I looked at my china in the bookcase, and my bits of silver and glass, but decided they would have to take their chance. I packed Great-grandy's miniature and the old christening robe that is so exquisitely embroidered, Great-grandy's snuffbox and Great-gran's card-case with its queer, shining, hand-written cards still in it – a few oddments for the boys, anyway.

I told my husband at lunchtime, and said, 'If you tell me what you would like me to put in this case, I'll pack it too – I've only got pyjamas, clean collars and handkerchiefs, and my nightdress and a change of undies.' We decided it was enough for a quick getaway, but in the corners I put all the papers that mattered, two unbreakable picnic cups, a spoon, a small bottle of Bovril, a small tin of milk, one of glucose, all the spare clean handkerchiefs, rolls of bandages, our stock of three-cornered bandages, scissors, aspirins, safety-pins and a tin-opener. My husband said laughingly, 'Fussy to the last' – and pointed to the two cups. He can never understand my odd way of liking my own towel, cup, comb etc. I suppose I am too fastidious – but it's just how I'm made and it's there. He said, 'I'm glad you are having forethought. If you saw the poor bewildered evacuees downtown, you would laugh and cry together. One woman carried a bowl of goldfish and could carry nothing else, there were blankets in which cheap trashy ornaments were packed instead of food or clothes, and a woman had a baby in a pram and a cage of moulty-looking canaries – instead of blankets, or clothes for the baby, and so on.' He went on, 'Now don't you come downtown – you would have to walk one way, if not both, and you couldn't do anything: all the Services are working like clockwork together, and you look all-in today!' It was only common sense – if I'd gone into town, it would only have been as a sightseer, and they can always be done without.

Thursday, 17 April

The noise of guns and bombs has put my three laying

hens off a little, but my sitting hen is firm and cosy on her clutch of pot eggs. I hope she keeps on till the chicks come. The poor little canary is dead. I don't like birds in cages, but my husband does, and he was sorry it died.

At the whist drive, I heard that long queues had formed at the outgoing bus stands – hundreds who were going to Dalton and Ulverston, five and ten miles away. Many took taxis, private cars were loaded, and those who could not get in a bus or taxi walked the five miles. There were, of course, no extra buses. It made me wonder what would happen if a big blitz or invasion occurred, and whether the 'Stay put' order would be any use – or would people throng the roads as they did in France? My husband said, 'I think we would take a chance and try to get to Spark Bridge, but I said, 'Please yourself – I stay. This is my home and these are my animals, and I'll stand by it and them. You must do as you think fit.' He said, 'What good is your home and your animals if you lose your life?' and I replied, 'What good is my life if I lose all I hold dear, even the feeling of respect for myself.' Perhaps I *am* mad, but as long as I've a corner to shelter me, and my work at the Centre, and have somewhere for the boys to think of still as home, I'll ask no more.

Wednesday, 8 August 1945

We talked about the atomic bomb. It seems to have frightened Mrs Howson very much. Our talk had a very Wellsian turn. We wondered if it was at all possible for German scientists to be hiding anywhere, and if they could send a revenge plane to wreck England – or American cities! We followed our fantastic themes of super 'werewolves' till we felt dizzy and were rather scared. This atomic bomb business is so dreadful. Was it something like this that happened when Atlantis disappeared under the sea, and the Age of Mythology began?

I cooked tea after she had gone. My husband was very late and was glad of a cooked meal. We had a good gardening evening. The garden is a glory of antirrhinums, sweetpeas and big clumps of white daisies, though the roses are not doing so well in the dry weather.

Tuesday 14 August
1.00 a.m.

I woke with a start from my half-awakeness, slightly alarmed at the shouting and noise of ships' sirens and church bells. Then I realised the longed-for news of peace had come through on the last news. I got out of bed and looked through the window. Cars were rushing down Abbey Road into the town. My neighbour, Mrs Helm, who is very excitable, was half-screaming 'God Save the King', seemingly knowing all the verses or singing what she did know over and over again. I remembered her words that she had a bottle of champagne and one of gin, and intended opening them both and drinking a tumbler full of each! My husband woke and came in. He said, 'Sounds as if it's all over.' Children's voices came from open bedroom windows; everywhere was chatter and noise, the sound of opening doors and people telling each other they had been in bed and asleep. I went into the back room and looked out over the town. I could see by the glow that bonfires had been lit. Rockets and searchlights went up from all the ships in the dock, and there were sounds of feet hurrying as if to go and see all that there was to be seen. Mrs Helm sounded as if she had done as she intended, and her daughter and son-in-law rushed up in their car – both seemed to be 'well lit up': they are the type who howl and shriek if they are happy – or sad. They all sounded as if they were letting themselves go.

My husband has gone back to bed, wishing there was not so much noise. I don't feel like getting dressed and going out myself, either. Even the dogs are barking crazily, as if the fireworks and noise have excited them. The ships' hooters seem to have been turned on and forgotten, and now the sound of fireworks is coming out of little back gardens, and there are shrill childish voices and shrieks from older girls, as if fire crackers are being tossed round.

I feel disappointed in my feelings. I feel no wild whoopee, just a quiet thankfulness and a feeling of 'flatness'. Dear God knows what I'd imagined it would be like. I think I'll take two aspirins and try and read myself to sleep.

Prison of the Soul

Jimmy Boyle

Jimmy Boyle was born in Glasgow in 1944. He was sent to prison for murder in 1967 and in 1972 was transferred to the new Special Unit at Barlinnie Prison. He was released in 1982. The extracts in this book come from the diary he wrote during that time. In them he reflects on his predicament and ponders the hope that he will be released eventually. The final extract records the moment of freedom.

28 May 1967   *Barlinnie Prison*

Looking around me as I sit locked in my cell with the natural light pouring in through the window, I think of how last week I thought of this week and how it would be the same. It is. Now look and think and see the barbarity of it. The lock shut tight alone in the early evening – it's not as though I would be a lonely person by choice. I am a private person who likes to retain his own identity but this is an imposed solitude. I think of the image of the past and how it is no longer me, yet it hangs around me, clinging. I look at the barbed wire that hangs outside my window and want to throw myself at it, not to climb over but as a gesture of defiance. It wouldn't be meant as a gesture of self-destruction though that would be the obvious consequence. It would be more a cry to humanity, to the people of the world as to what they are doing. It's all about these very strong passionate and very tender feelings deep within that have been buried for so long, that have been expressed in snide ways. I always knew they existed but didn't know what they were or what they meant. Having gained this knowledge and having learned a lot about my life and society, I feel my earlier life has been stolen from me.

29 May

Last night I went to bed at 8.35 p.m. as I couldn't face looking at the cell walls, doors and windows. I felt exhausted and was soon sound asleep. This morning I wakened and went outside to do my running exercises. While doing so I thought, in the freshness of the morning, of my thoughts of the night before. I thought of the soil and my returning to it. It's inevitable at some point, and the daily struggle in here has reached a level where I am facing each day in a condition of rawness, where exposure to the actual surroundings is excruciatingly painful. Strangely enough the one moment of respite I got this morning was when I lifted a 400 lb weight. I don't know why but somehow the heavy weight matched what I felt. I showered, shaved and dressed. While doing so I looked at myself in the mirror. I looked very healthy and thought of how the external belies the internal...

This afternoon my aunt Peggy and cousin came to visit me bringing my two children, James and Patricia, with them. I put on a 'mask' and sat with them, but it was flat, and yet I felt so terribly close to them. I managed to get my children away on their own and have a chat with them. Here I am in this situation just as in previous nights. Is it this, or am I using the confinement as an excuse to avoid the deeper issues lying inside me? Why do I feel as though all that is inside me is blocked in my throat? I feel the best thing I can do is to remain away from everyone for a day or two till I work this thing through. Thank God for the music that is playing – a Brandenburg Concerto.

There was a time when the things that now hurt me never would have as I would have been too insensitive to them. Therefore, is sensitivity a bad thing in a situation, or, more to the point, in a world such as this? No, the answer must be no.

2 January 1978

3.14 a.m. I've been wakened for over an hour, am irritable and restless. The Radio Clyde disc jockey is speaking to people in their homes via telephone. I get the atmosphere of home parties from it. Pop music is blasting in my ears and I marvel at radio and how it must comfort lonely people. It's almost as though it's reassuring me I'm not alone. 3.55 a.m. One of these days I won't be 'still here'. It's amazing how difficult I find it to think of myself being anywhere else.

26 October 1981

Stepping across the gate into Sarah's arms. We embrace and kiss. So lovely to touch in legitimate time. We waste no time jumping in the car and heading into the distance.

Accumulated thoughts: I am wondering what it will be like to sleep together, having known each other for four years and been married almost two. Up the long winding roads the scenery was spectacular. Sitting there with Sarah at my side, the prison far behind and the wonders of the Scottish Highlands all around me I felt stunned with pleasure... How can I possibly explain this experience to anyone after fourteen years in prison? Every fibre was open and alert to this vast mountain scenery. Finally we reached our caravan situated high up on the hillside with a wide and full view of the valley. It was getting quite dark though still enough light for us to see our view from the caravan. Sheep were all around us. We looked down the valley to a spattering of cottages and farmhouses. The visual images were overwhelming. The night was spent in a small double bed with me always aware of Sarah next to me. I was restless. It will take some getting used to after fourteen years of sleeping alone ... It's the first time in years I've slept on a mattress.

A Break from the House

Alan Clark

Alan Clark has published diaries which cover the period from 1983 to 1991, during which time he was Conservative MP for Plymouth, Minister of Trade and later Minister of State in the Ministry of Defence. His diary throws an interesting light on the politics of the period but also contains personal and family events. It is, he insists, 'a real diary'. This extract records a time when he was able to take time out from his busy schedule (and the 'Boxes') as a member of Margaret Thatcher's government. He mentions the guide he wrote to Seend parish church, his opposition to the modernised version of the Anglican prayer book and the old walled garden which he and his wife Jane kept after selling the Manor House.

Friday, 31 August 1984

I called in at Seend this morning, on my way back from the West Country, and said a prayer in the church – must be one of the few remaining where the vicar obligingly leaves the door open.

It's too frustrating, I can now only get this sense of peace, and of communication – something of the confessional, I suppose – in empty churches. There, in the silence, through which I can hear the whisperings of gossip and desire, the intoned devotions of two, three centuries, I feel tranquil. Strangely, I should think I have prayed here more often since we left, than in all the time that we lived in the village.

I was glad to see that the Guide, which I wrote, at Archie Kidd's insistence, with dear old 'Mr Wiltshire' (yes, I have to keep reminding myself, the sage of Wiltshire was actually *called* 'Wiltshire') is still on offer in the racks.

But no proper Bible, or King James' Prayer Book. I am completely certain that this degradation of the ancient form and language is a calculated act, a deliberate subversion by a hard core whose secret purpose is to distort the beliefs and practices of the Church of England.

Every time – usually by accident – that I attend a service where 'Series III' is used, and suffer that special jarring pain when (most often in the Responses) a commonplace illiteracy, straight out of a local authority circular, supplants the beautiful, numinous phrases on which I was brought up and from which I drew comfort for thirty-five years, my heart sinks. All too well do I understand the rage of the *Inquisitadores*.[1] I would gladly burn them, those trendy clerics, at the stake. What fun to hear them pinkly squealing. Or perhaps, as the faggots kindled, they would 'come out', and call on the Devil to succour them.

The 'Secret Garden' is now totally overgrown and the glasshouses lush and tropical with unpicked grapes and fireweed. The big green double gates still batteredly leaning, done up with baling twine, just as we left them when, two years ago, we called by to load the Range Rover with apples. The whole flavour of the place a little more remote, now twelve years or more away, and through a glass darkly. I climbed over the wall from the churchyard, trying not to put too much weight on the

[1] officials of the Spanish Inquisition who tried people for crimes against the Church

rickety corrugated iron roof of the Gravedigger's hut. A beautiful orange dogfox, as big as a setter, ran out of the potting shed and slithered away into the undergrowth, like Sredni Vashtar.[2] A good sanctuary, the hounds will never find him there. The key for the Marley store was still under its usual stone and I let myself in, prowled about for a little while, collected some Bentley bits, yet still got to Chippenham in time to catch the 10.08 to Paddington and the Boxes.

[2] an animal in a story by Saki (H. H. Munro) which was kept in a garden shed

In a Place of Hidden Danger

Michael Palin

Michael Palin was a member of the comic Monty Python team and is now an actor, TV presenter and writer. He made his journey from North to South Poles along the 30° East line of longitude between July and Christmas 1991. His account of it is based on tape recordings of events 'as they happened' as well as on a diary kept throughout. It was published as *Pole to Pole*. Travelling south from the North Pole, Michael Palin has already seen the splendours of Helsinki and St Petersburg (then called Leningrad). This day's log records an apprehensively made detour near to the site of the world's worst nuclear disaster, which happened at Chernobyl in the Ukraine in 1986.

Day 35 1991

Today we are going close to Chernobyl to visit towns and villages that have been, or are about to be, evacuated as a result of the disaster. We shall not be entering the 30-mile exclusion zone but will be in contaminated areas and Volodya, Irena and the rest of our Russian team will not be coming with us. Mirabel too has decided not to risk it. Roger has been in contact with the National Radiological Protection Board at Harwell, whose advice offered mixed comfort. They said radiation levels would be the same, if not less, than at the Poles, with their concentration of magnetic forces. However, the knowledge that there is still confusion and debate over the effects of the disaster, and the advice from scientists that we wear shoes and clothing we could throw away afterwards adds a frisson of danger to the journey, and there is some nervous joking over the slivers of cheese at breakfast.

We head north and west from Kiev, making for the town of Narodichi. It's 42 miles due west of Chernobyl, two of whose reactors, Vadim reminds us, are still operational. The Ukrainian Parliament has voted unanimously to close them down. The Soviet government has refused. The Ukrainians claim 8000 died as a result of the accident. The official Soviet figure is 32.

We are passing through woodlands of pine and oak scrub interspersed with harvested fields and cherry and almond orchards. An army convoy of 40 trucks passes, heading south. After a while the woodland gives way to a wide and fertile agricultural plain. The first indication that this abundance is tainted comes as quite a shock. It's a sign, set in brambles and long grass, which reads, 'Warning: It is forbidden for cattle to graze, and to gather mushrooms, strawberries and medicinal herbs.'

We stop here and put on our yellow TLD badges, which register radiation levels, and which will be sent back to Harwell for analysis after our three-hour visit. Armed with these and a radiation detector, we enter Narodichi where people have lived with radiation for over five years. It's a neat, proud little town with a chestnut-lined main street and a silver-painted Lenin in front of the party headquarters. In a year's time there will be no one here.

In the municipal gardens the grass is uncut but a fountain still plays. There are several memorials. One is a scorched tree with a cross on it – local people think that the forest protected them from the worst of the blast. Beside the tree are three large boulders, one of which commemorates four villages and 548 people evacuated in 1986, another 15 villages and 3264 people evacuated in 1990. Twenty-two more villages and a further 11,000 people will be going in 1991. An inscription read: 'In memory of the villages and human destinies of the Narodichi region burnt down by radiation.'

One of the most polluted areas is the children's playground, with 13 to 17 times normal gamma radiation levels. The red metal chairs hang down from the roundabout and blue steel boats swing gently in the breeze, but no one is allowed to play here anymore.

Michael, the local schoolmaster, is short and podgy and his face is an unhealthy grey. There were 10,000 children in the region, he tells me, now there are 3000. Two of his pupils pass by on bicycles and he grabs them and introduces us. The boys, just back from a Pioneer camp in Poland, look bored, and reply in monosyllables, which Michael translates thus: 'The children send fraternal greetings to children throughout the United Kingdom.' He smiles proudly and a little desperately. I ask if the children's work has been affected by their proximity to Chernobyl. He sighs and nods.

'There is not a single healthy child here.'

As we drive out of Narodichi, Michael talks proudly of the history of his town, interspersing this with casually chilling present-day observations.

'This is the bridge over the Oush river. It is area of highest pollution.'

We come to the village of Nozdrishche, which was evacuated last year. There are no ruins, there is no devastation or destruction. Wooden cottages with painted window-frames stand in their orderly rows. Flowers are in bloom and grasshoppers dart around in lush overgrown gardens. It is a hot, soft, gentle summer's day. Yet scientists who have visited the area say it could be 700 years before this place comes back to life. It is hard to know what to believe, for whatever curse lies over these villages is the more frightening for being invisible. It is how one has heard the countryside would be after a nuclear war – benign, smiling, deadly.

A year's exposure to the weather has not yet dissipated a faint smell of disinfectant in a small, deserted maternity hospital. A poster on the wall depicts the American space shuttle spinning round the earth, with the single word 'Nyet!' beneath. There is a book on breastfeeding, its leaves nibbled by mice, an examination chair, medical records still in files, and a portrait of Lenin which has fallen out of its frame and lies in a corner beneath a scattering of glass slides and syringes. Conscious of the limited time we have been advised to spend here we move on through the village. I catch sight of two figures down a lane to one side of the main street. One is a very old lady, whose name is Heema, and the other her nephew. Heema is 90 years old and has refused to be moved from the village. She says she has been moved five times since the disaster and now she is too old and ill. Her one wish is to die in the house in which she was born, but that is now cordoned off with barbed wire, so she will remain here with her daughter. They are the only inhabitants of Nozdrishche.

Further along the road, at the village of Novoye Sharno, the radiation detector bleeps for the first time.

'Pay attention, please,' says Michael, 'the radiation is very high here.'

This is one of the villages evacuated in 1986, immediately after the explosion and fire, and the village shop is now almost submerged in the undergrowth. Inside it is a mess of broken shelves, abandoned goods, smashed bottles.

'There was a panic here,' Vadim explains, unnecessarily.

We drive back through Narodichi, where, as in Novoye Sharno and Nozdrishche and over 40 villages in this region alone, the grass will soon grow around doors that will never be opened again, and anyone who comes here will be informed of the dangers and the risks which those who lived here were not told about until it was too late.

Back in Kiev, two and a half hours later, I'm struck once again by the spruceness of the city compared to Leningrad or Novgorod. A Russian, writing in the *Insight Guide*, relates even this to Chernobyl: 'The terrible effects of the tragedy made many people, in Kiev and other towns, take another look at themselves. Kiev is cleaner, and not merely because the streets are watered twice a day now; once the people were shown the frailty of human existence, they changed.'

We end up the day in a brick-vaulted cellar in the Andreevsky Spusk, a Montmartre-like street full of cafes and shops and predominantly student meeting places. The food is the best we've had in the Soviet Union – Armenian–Georgian cooking – kebabs, rabbit stew, aubergine and onion salad. An excellent jazz trio of bass, fiddle and piano plays local music and well-served-up classics like 'Take the A-Train'. Vodka flows freely. It is one of the best evenings, and in a sense, the only way of dealing with what we have seen today.

A Child in Wartime

Zlata Filipovic

Zlata Filipovic first showed her diary to a teacher and it was
published in Sarajevo with the help of UNICEF. She became a
celebrity overnight against a background of war. On 23
December 1993 she and her parents were able to leave
Sarajevo and they now live in Paris. Zlata began her diary in
September 1991. She soon found herself recording the events
of a bloody civil war between the peoples of former
Yugoslavia. Here we see how an ordinary eleven-year-old tries
to hold on to her childhood through the ravages of war on her
home town of Sarajevo.

Tuesday, 14 January 1992

I yawned, opened my pen and started to write: I'm
listening to the music from *Top Gun* on Good Vibrations
(on the radio). Something else is on now. I've just
destroyed the back page of *Bazar* [a fashion magazine].
I talked to Mummy on the phone. She's at work.

I have something to tell you. Every night I dream that
I'm asking Michael Jackson for his autograph, but
either he won't give it to me or his secretary writes it,
and then all the letters melt, because Michael Jackson
didn't write them. Sad. Poor me. Ha, ha, ha, ha, I have
to, ha, ha, ha, ha, laugh, ha, ha, ha, ha.

16.15. I was at Vanja's and Andrej's (V&A). There was
a bit of trouble at home because I stayed so long. But it
took a long time to finish our game of Monopoly. Both

Vanja and Andrej went bankrupt, and I had all the red notes (5,000 each). I had 12,000,000, to be exact. Mind you, I had the Place de Genève and Côte d'Azur.

Oops. There's Bugs Bunny. I've got to watch!

19.50. I'm watching DIAL MTV:

5. Pet Shop Boys with 'Was It Worth It?'
4. I can't remember
3. Nirvana
2. Guns n' Roses
1. New Kids on the Block.

Thursday, 5 March

Oh, God! Things are heating up in Sarajevo. On Sunday (1 March), a small group of armed civilians (as they say on TV) killed a Serbian wedding guest and wounded the priest. On 2 March (Monday) the whole city was full of barricades. There were '1,000' barricades. We didn't even have bread. At 18.00 people got fed up and went out into the streets. The procession set out from the cathedral. It went past the parliament building and made its way through the entire city. Several people were wounded at the Marshal Tito army barracks. People sang and cried 'Bosnia, Bosnia', 'Sarajevo, Sarajevo', 'We'll live together' and 'Come and join us'. Zdravko Grebo said on the radio that history was in the making.

At about 20.00 we heard the bell of a tram. The first tram had passed through town and life got back to normal. People poured out into the streets hoping that nothing like that would ever happen again. We joined the peace procession. When we got home we had a quiet night's sleep. The next day everything was the same as before. Classes, music school... But in the evening, the news came that 3,000 Chetniks [Serbian nationalists] were coming from Pale to attack Sarajevo, and first, Baščaršija [the old part of town]. Melica said that new barricades had been put up in front of her house and that they wouldn't be sleeping at home tonight. They went to Uncle Nedjad's place. Later there was a real row on YUTEL TV. Radovan Karadžič [Bosnian Serb leader] and Alija Izetbegovič [President of Bosnia-Herzegovina] phoned in and started arguing. Then Goran Milic got angry and made them agree to meet with some General Kukanjac. Milič is great!!! Bravo!

On 4 March (Wednesday) the barricades were removed, the 'kids' [a popular term for politicians] had come to some agreement. Great?!

That day our art teacher brought in a picture for our class-mistress (for 8 March, Women's Day). We gave her the present, but she told us to go home. Something was wrong again! There was a panic. The girls started screaming and the boys quietly blinked their eyes. Daddy came home from work early that day too. But everything turned out OK. It's all too much!

Friday, 6 March

Things are back to normal.

Monday, 30 March

Hey, Diary! You know what I think? Since Anne Frank called her diary Kitty, maybe I could give you a name too. What about:

ASFALTINA	PICŽAMETA
ŠEFIKA	HIKMETA
ŠEVALA	MIMMY

or something else???

I'm thinking, thinking . . .

I've decided! I'm going to call you

MIMMY

All right, then, let's start.

Dear Mimmy,

It's almost half-term. We're all studying for our tests. Tomorrow we're supposed to go to a classical music concert at the Skenderija Hall. Our teacher says we shouldn't go because there will be 10,000 people, pardon me, children, there, and somebody might take us as hostages or plant a bomb in the concert hall. Mummy says I shouldn't go. So I won't.

Hey! You know who won the Yugovision Song Contest?! EXTRA NENA!!!???

I'm afraid to say this next thing. Melica says she heard at the hairdresser's that on Saturday, 4 April 1992, there's going to be BOOM-BOOM, BANG-BANG, CRASH Sarajevo. Translation: they're going to bomb Sarajevo.

Love,
Zlata

Thursday, 9 April

Dear Mimmy,

I'm not going to school. All the schools in Sarajevo are closed. There's danger hiding in these hills above Sarajevo. But I think things are slowly calming down. The heavy shelling and explosions have stopped. There's occasional gunfire, but it quickly falls silent. Mummy and Daddy aren't going to work. They're buying food in huge quantities. Just in case, I guess. God forbid!

Still, it's very tense. Mummy is beside herself, Daddy tries to calm her down. Mummy has long conversations on the phone. She calls, other people call, the phone is in constant use.

ZLATA

Saturday, 2 May

Dear Mimmy,

Today was truly, absolutely the worst day ever in Sarajevo. The shooting started around noon. Mummy and I moved into the hall. Daddy was in his office, under our flat, at the time. We told him on the interphone to run quickly to the downstairs lobby where we'd meet him. We brought Cicko [Zlata's canary] with us. The gunfire was getting worse, and we couldn't get over the wall to the Bobars, so we ran down to our own cellar.

The cellar is ugly, dark, smelly. Mummy, who's terrified of mice, had two fears to cope with. The three of us were in the same corner as the other day. We listened to the pounding shells, the shooting, the thundering noise overhead. We even heard planes. At one moment I realised that this awful cellar was the only place that could save our lives. Suddenly, it started to look almost warm and nice. It was the only way we could defend ourselves against all this terrible shooting. We heard glass shattering in our street. Horrible. I put my fingers in my ears to block out the terrible sounds. I was worried about Cicko. We had left him behind in the lobby. Would he catch cold there? Would something hit him? I was terribly hungry and thirsty. We had left our half-cooked lunch in the kitchen.

When the shooting died down a bit, Daddy ran over to our flat and brought us back some sandwiches. He said he could smell something burning and that the phones weren't working. He brought our TV set down to the cellar. That's when we learned that the main post office (near us) was on fire and that they had kidnapped our President. At around 20.00 we went back up to our flat. Almost every window in our street was broken. Ours were all right, thank God. I saw the post office in flames. A terrible sight. The fire-fighters battled with the raging fire. Daddy took a few photos of the post office being devoured by the flames. He said they wouldn't come out because I had been fiddling with something on the camera. I was sorry. The whole flat smelled of the burning fire. God, and I used to pass by there every day. It had just been done up. It was huge and beautiful, and now it was being swallowed up by the flames. It was disappearing. That's what this neighbourhood of mine looks like, dear Mimmy. I wonder what it's like in other parts of town? I heard on the radio that it was awful around the Eternal Flame. The place is knee-deep in glass. We're worried about Grandma and Grandad. They live there. Tomorrow, if we can go out, we'll see how they are. A terrible day. This has been the worst, most awful day in my eleven-year-old life. I hope it will be the only one.

Mummy and Daddy are very edgy. I have to go to bed.

Ciao!
ZLATA

Sunday, 3 May

Dear Mimmy,
Daddy managed to run across the bridge over the

Miljacka and get to Grandma and Grandad. He came running back, all upset, sweating with fear and sadness. They're all right, thank God. Tito Street looks awful. The heavy shelling has destroyed shop windows, cars, flats, the fronts and roofs of buildings. Luckily, not too many people were hurt because they managed to take shelter. Neda (Mummy's girlfriend) rushed over to see how we were and to tell us that they were OK and hadn't had any damage. But it was terrible.

We talked through the window with Auntie Boda and Bojana just now. They were in the street yesterday when that heavy shooting broke out. They managed to get to Stela's cellar.

ZLATA

Tuesday, 5 May

Dear Mimmy,
The shooting seems to be dying down. I guess they've caused enough misery, although I don't know why. It has something to do with politics. I just hope the 'kids' come to some agreement. Oh, if only they would, so we could live and breathe as human beings again. The things that have happened here these past few days are terrible. I want it to stop for ever. PEACE! PEACE!

I didn't tell you, Mimmy, that we've rearranged things in the flat. My room and Mummy's and Daddy's are too dangerous to be in. They face the hills, which is where they're shooting from. If only you knew how scared I am to go near the windows and into those rooms. So, we turned a safe corner of the sitting room into a 'bedroom'. We sleep on mattresses on the floor. It's strange and awful. But, it's safer that way. We've turned everything around for safety. We put Cicko in the kitchen. He's safe there, although once the shooting starts there's nowhere safe except the cellar. I suppose all this will stop and we'll all go back to our usual places.

Ciao!
ZLATA

Thursday, 7 May

Dear Mimmy,

I was almost positive the war would stop, but today... Today a shell fell on the park in front of my house, the park where I used to play with my girlfriends. A lot of people were hurt. From what I hear Jaca, Jaca's mother, Selma, Nina, our neighbour Dado and who knows how many other people who happened to be there were wounded. Dado, Jaca and her mother have come home from hospital, Selma lost a kidney but I don't know how she is, because she's still in hospital. AND NINA IS DEAD. A piece of shrapnel lodged in her brain and she died. She was such a sweet, nice little girl. We went to kindergarten together, and we used to play together in the park. Is it possible I'll never see Nina again? Nina, an innocent eleven-year-old little girl – the victim of a stupid war. I feel sad. I cry and wonder why? She didn't do anything. A disgusting war has destroyed a young child's life. Nina, I'll always remember you as a wonderful little girl.

Love, Mimmy,
ZLATA

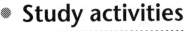

Study activities

Diaries

1 Keep a diary of your own for the period of one week.

You will obviously need to record some of the week's events in it and you can include your thoughts and feelings about them. Make a special effort, for the last few lines of each entry, to make a note of your experience of writing the diary itself. For example, you may find it very difficult to think of anything to say and suspect that no one would find it an interesting read. Or you may find that your pen runs away with you, or that you have so much to say that there is not time to write it all. You may experience all of these; each day is likely to be different.

2 After a week, use your diary and any of the diary extracts in this volume as material for discussion of the following ideas:

- What are the advantages of keeping a diary for oneself *and/or* for others to read? What disadvantages might there be? (See particularly Fanny Burney, Anne Frank, Zlata Filipovic, Samuel Pepys.)

- Consider the question of audience. Who is the diarist writing for *either* in general *or* in specific cases? (See Burney, Dorothy Wordsworth, James Boswell.)

- What motivates people to begin writing a diary? What motivates them to maintain it for long periods? (See Jimmy Boyle, Boswell, Wordsworth, Frank, Filipovic, Nella Last.)

- To what uses could people's diaries be put (whether they are published or not)? (Consider Pepys, Boswell, Wordsworth, Filipovic, Frank, Last, Alan Clark.)

3 You have been asked by the 'Literary Heritage Travel Bureau' to compile an itinerary and write an accompanying publicity brochure for the 'Wordsworth Tour' they are planning. Use Dorothy Wordsworth's diary and a good road atlas of the British Isles (such as the AA or RAC publish) or the relevant OS maps to help you. You may work alone or with a team of compilers and writers. Think carefully about:

- Modes of transport – will you consider recreating the Wordsworths' journey exactly or will you use modern transportation? If the latter, what will you include in your brochure to give tourists the right 'flavour' of the times?

- Accommodation – consider the number of overnight stops required and offer suitable lodging. You may wish to contact the English Tourist Board for information about places to stay, or you may be lucky enough to have suitable material in your local library. What meals will be provided?

- Entertainment – consider the type of person who might be interested in tracing the steps of the poet Wordsworth and design a programme of evening and (possibly) daytime entertainments that will suit them and reflect the literary theme of the tour. This will involve finding out a little more about Wordsworth and his work – use your library.

- Souvenirs – tourists usually like to take home some memento of their holiday. What kinds of items might you, the tour company, be able to offer them?

4 In times of catastrophe, war, or imprisonment human beings' basic needs come to the front of their thoughts. All of the following diarists mention things that they feel are essential to their survival or see others attempting to salvage or hoard: Anne Frank, Zlata Filipovic, Samuel Pepys and Jimmy Boyle. Read through all of these diary entries before you begin.

- In a group of four (or you could divide your whole class into four groups) take one diary each. Decide for that diarist what *they* would consider to be the ten most important things for survival when disaster strikes and list them. The list does not need to contain only material things.

- When all four lists are complete, bring the diarists together and (preferably with one person in role for each writer, although this is not essential) let each one describe their list. Others may question their choice and the diarist (and his or her group) must justify their decisions to include each item.

- Compile a definitive list of the ten most important things for human survival, bringing all the diarists to a consensus.

5 You have been contacted by a local television station and asked to prepare a taster episode for a serialisation of one of the diaries in this volume. The choice of diary is up to you. Decide whether you want to present something humorous (e.g. Boswell, Woodforde, Burney), exciting (e.g. Frank, Filipovic, Pepys), intellectual (e.g. Webb), or sad (e.g. Palin).

You could give yourself a better understanding of the diary by reading more of it. Although this is not strictly necessary for you to complete the activity which follows, you will find more knowledge helps you.

- Choose the incident you intend to use in your programme. Draw out a storyboard for it in not more than twelve frames.

- In keeping with the period of the writer, design a single set (although of course your whole episode may move location). This may require some research.

- Design costumes for the diarist and one other person mentioned in the diary. Again you may need to research details to keep them authentic to the period.

- Music, both for the title sequence and as incidental music, is important to any televisation. Listen to music from the appropriate period and choose one or two pieces, saying when you would like them to be heard within the episode.

- Casting will be essential to this serial. Suggest current actors who might suit the roles of diarist and other personalities perfectly.

- The screenplay or script is the most important part of your work here. Stay as faithful as you can to the diary, but include additional dialogue where you feel this will help your audience understand what is happening. Will you consider using voice-over technique to give the diarist's thoughts, or have you a different idea for this?

- Review your work and assess whether or not you have managed to a) keep the tone of the piece and b) make it clear that this is a diary and not a novel or autobiography. If you are in any doubt about these two points, edit your submission.

6 Devise a news report for a local or national newspaper, or script a report for TV or radio, based on the events which are recorded in any of the diaries you have read.

- The event you choose to report on must, of course, be newsworthy for the medium you select. National media would aim to give information to the whole country about such events as disasters (such as the Great Fire of London – Pepys), wars (air-raids on a major ship-building town – Nella Last), or the private lives of celebrities (the wedding of Queen Victoria). Local media would also be interested in reporting the death of a local person (Vera Brittain's fiancé) or the visit of a VIP (Dr Johnson in Skye, from Boswell's diary).

- Consider the style, audience and effect of your writing according to the news you choose to report. You may wish to use an 'authentic' or appropriate style such as a broadsheet newspaper for eighteenth-century events, a wireless report of World War II bombing, or a television news format for Zlata's diary events. Alternatively you could experiment with forms of media communication which would not necessarily have been available at the time the diary was written.

7 Read Alan Clark's diary as an example of how revisiting a place can trigger memories, remind us of things we have learnt, or incite us to explore our opinions about issues that matter to us personally. Then write your own 'diary entry' for a visit, exploring the ideas you associate with the place, as well as describing the event in detail.

8 Read Beatrice and Sidney Webb's diary.

a) Make notes on the position of women in society in 1912, in India and in Britain. You may wish to do further research into the suffragette movement and the historical context of the diary before you begin. You could also read the diaries of Queen Victoria, Samuel Pepys and Zlata as contrasts from other historical periods.

b) Consider the statement: 'All rulers should be women' and argue your point of view on this matter in essay form as clearly as you are able. You may use both historical and contemporary examples of female and male rulers to carry your arguments.

Letters

1 Despatches, or short clear communications, are important to those involved in military activities, as can be seen in the letters written by Charles I and Prince Rupert. Imagine that you are the recipient of one (or both) of these letters and write your reply. You must make it extremely clear what you are going to do in each case. Will you offer reassurance or suggest that there are further problems? You may choose to use a style similar to that of the seventeenth-century writers or a modern, telegrammatic style.

2 Sir John Harington's letter appears to have been written purely for the amusement of Prince Henry. Write a letter describing the virtues, or even the failings, of a particular pet with the purpose of amusing and entertaining the reader. Your intended correspondent does not need to be of royal blood!

3 Sir Ernest Shackleton had not seen his daughter for two years when he wrote the letter in this volume. Like Michael Hewat, his occupation kept him away from those he loved for long periods. Decide upon a person you have not seen for some time. This need not be a relative. You may well be able to think of a friend who has left your area to live somewhere else, or you may have moved yourself. Perhaps you have neglected your penfriend or your foreign-exchange partner recently. Write a letter to that person to update them on how you are. It need not be a 'wish you were here' letter but you might suggest things to do when you next meet. Once your letter is written, make a good copy of it and send it.

4 Read Jane Austen's letters to her niece, Fanny Knight, carefully several times over.

a) Make a list of the main points of advice that she offers in each letter. Compare the two and decide whether she is consistent in what she recommends.

b) Discuss the advice with others and think about whether it is
   • good advice for Fanny
   • good advice for young women today
   • good advice for young people in general.

c) *Either* prepare a letter to Fanny Knight offering a twentieth-century perspective,
   Or write a letter to a younger person offering advice on love, school work, careers, how to cope with parents or anything else which you feel would be useful to them. (You might also read Fanny Burney's diary before you do this, particularly the section where Miss Young advises her over the writing of journals.)

5 News will on the whole fall into one of two categories: good news or bad news. Read any, or all, of the letters by Charlotte Brontë, Thomas Carlyle, Horatio Nelson, Michael Hewat and P.G. Wodehouse and decide into which category they fall.

a) For any of the above write a letter in response to what you have read, offering condolences or congratulations as appropriate.

b) Compile a list of ideas for happy events and bad news based on your experience and that of friends or family. Choose one idea from each category and write letters (the choice of recipient is yours) which break the news in appropriate and sensitive ways. You could also write a letter in response. If you do so, consider the reactions of the recipient (P.G. Wodehouse's second letter and Vera Brittain's diary entry will help you here).

c) Alternatively you could consider the experiences of one of the characters in a work of fiction you have recently read, either as a class or alone. Writing as if you are a character from the book or play write a letter to another character sending news of one kind. Give this to someone else who has read the book or play and ask them to write a letter which reacts to the news. For example, Macbeth might write to his wife about the death of MacDuff's wife and children, and she would then reply.

Overview

1 Compare any *two* (or more if you wish) of the following pieces of writing about the business of travel: James Boswell, Dorothy Wordsworth, Michael Palin, Lady Mary Wortley Montagu, Sir Ernest Shackleton.

   a) Which of your chosen pieces do you consider to be the more: factual? exciting? amusing? disturbing?

   b) How far were your decisions on the above influenced by: the writer's style? chosen form? subject matter?

   c) Write a detailed critique of *one* of the chosen pieces, outlining your preferences. Make reference to the other piece(s) you have studied and compare them. End your work by explaining as clearly as possible why you would recommend *one* of the pieces more highly than the others to a modern reader.

2 Read the pieces in this collection written by Charles I, Prince Rupert, Horatio Nelson, Vera Brittain, Michael Hewat, Nella Last, Anne Frank and Zlata Filipovic. Compare the reaction and response to war of any *three* of these writers, spanning at least two different wars.

3 Make a language study across this collection of writers. Choosing at least *one* diarist or letter writer from each century represented note down your observations on how written English has changed since 1608 under the headings 'Grammar and sentence construction', 'Vocabulary or choice of words,' 'Tone', 'Style and formality'.

You could slant your choice of writers deliberately to allow a study of how words have changed their meaning over time or become obsolete. You could examine the use of slang (informal or non-standard words or phrases, such as 'blow-out' meaning a large meal) or cliché (unoriginal or over-used phrases such as 'history was in the making'). Some other features of language might also suggest themselves to you.

Present your findings about language as an informative talk or written in the style of an encyclopaedia entry.

● Further reading

Diaries

The Diary of John Evelyn selected and edited by J. Bowle
(Oxford University Press, 1983)
Evelyn's diaries were discovered in the nineteenth century,
hidden in an old clothes basket in the house where he died
over a hundred years before. The diary runs from 1641
until his death in 1706 and is a fascinating source of
information on his life and times.

The Journal of Beatrix Potter from 1881 to 1897 edited by
Leslie Linder (Warne, 1966)
Beatrix Potter, more famous for her series of books for
children, was an avid diarist and left several books of
diaries. Like Pepys she wrote her journals in cipher and
these were not finally decoded until the 1960s.

The Journal of a Country Parish by Robin Page (Oxford
University Press, 1986)
Working as a village postman for a year brought Page into
contact with all the realities of country life. This book paints
a charming picture of twentieth-century rural life.

The Faber Book of Diaries edited by Simon Brett (Faber,
1987)
An excellent bedside book, packed with the highlights of
the lives of many diarists from the reign of Mary I to the
present day.

Letters

Letters Home by Sylvia Plath, edited by A.S. Plath (Faber, 1975)
The poet Sylvia Plath wrote many letters to her mother both from college in her native country, America, and from England as the young wife of Ted Hughes. They contain all the variety of pathos and humour also found in her poetry.

Dearest Beatie, My Darling Jack: A Victorian Couple's Love Letters edited by Rosalie Vicars-Harris and David Fordham (Collins, 1983)
This is a touching and authentic collection of letters written between 1898 and 1899. Both intimate and domestic, the real lives of the correspondents shine through.

The Faber Book of Letters edited by Felix Pryor (Faber, 1988)
An excellent collection for dipping and browsing.

The First Cuckoo: Letters to The Times since 1900 chosen by Kenneth Gregory (Unwin, 1976)
Witty and amusing letters on a large range of subjects which were originally published on the letters page of *The Times* newspaper.

Fiction

The collection in this volume has been selected on the grounds that all its contents should be the actual diaries and letters of real people. Over the centuries, however, there have been forgeries and fictional diaries, and novels written in an 'epistolary' form (i.e. as if they were a series of letters). Below are some suggested titles.

Diary and journal form

A Journal of the Plague Year (1722) by Daniel Defoe
Written as if it were a day-to-day account of the year 1665, Defoe's journal contains convincing naturalistic detail of a terrifying epidemic. This makes an interesting read alongside Pepys's diary which was written at the time and the diary of John Evelyn.

The Diary of a Nobody (1892) by George and Weedon Grossmith
Mr Pooter tells of his life in London. In him we recognise at least one person we know, and laugh at every episode. Compare his antics with those of Reverend Woodforde.

Z for Zachariah by Robert C. O'Brien (Lions,1976)
Ann Burden is the only survivor of a nuclear disaster; at least she thinks she is until the appearance of the menacing Mr Loomis.

The Secret Diary of Adrian Mole aged thirteen and three quarters by Sue Townsend (Methuen, 1983)
Well-known and loved, this is the first of the hilarious Adrian diaries. A love-sick teenager, he contrasts sharply with the seriousness of Anne Frank or Zlata.

The Remains of the Day by Kazuo Ishiguro (Faber, 1989)
Winner of the 1989 Booker Prize, this is the holiday diary of
a butler, Stevens. He has a great deal to tell us; should we
believe all he writes?

Fictional letter collections and epistolary novels

Pamela (1740) by Samuel Richardson
Recognised by many as the first-ever epistolary novel, this
book has a serious moral purpose. It was later mimicked
and mocked by Henry Fielding in his book *Joseph Andrews*
and in *Tom Jones*.

Lady Susan (written 1793–4) by Jane Austen
This is one of the lesser-known novels of Jane Austen, for
even she found the medium of the epistolary novel difficult
to sustain. However, it makes an interesting comparison
with her non-fictional letters.

Further reading projects

1 Read Dr Johnson's *A Journey to the Western Islands of
Scotland* and compare any passages of it with the
corresponding ones in Boswell's *The Journal of a Tour to the
Hebrides*. How can you account for the differences, stylistic
and in the selection of material, between these two
accounts of the same tour?

2 Read William Wordsworth's sonnet 'On Westminster Bridge' and Dorothy's diary entry in this collection. How much has the poet gleaned from his sister's record of their visit to London? What do you find especially striking about the way in which the poet has chosen to use the material and add to it?

Upon Westminster Bridge

3 September 1802

Earth has not anything to show more fair:
Dull would he be of soul who could pass by
A sight so touching in its majesty:
This City now doth like a garment wear
The beauty of the morning; silent, bare,
Ships, towers, domes, theatres, and temples lie
Open unto the fields, and to the sky,
All bright and glittering in the smokeless air.

Never did sun more beautifully steep

In his first splendour valley, rock, or hill;
Ne'er saw I, never felt, a calm so deep!

The river glideth at his own sweet will:
Dear God! the very houses seem asleep;
And all that mighty heart is lying still!

3 Read any of the diary extracts from this collection plus one other of your own choice (from Further reading list or otherwise). From your reading write a study entitled 'The appeal of the diary'.

4 Read any of the letters from this collection and a selection of others (from the Further reading list or otherwise). From your reading write an essay in which you argue the case for or against 'The telephone – destroyer of the art of letter-writing'.

5 Using either diaries or letters, read some authentic and some fictional materials. Choose a good example (perhaps written by the same person e.g. Jane Austen or Fanny Burney, or about the same century e.g. Pepys and Defoe) of each to show *either*

a) that it is impossible to tell when something is fact and when it is fiction, *or*

b) that it is always easy to spot authentic historical writing.

Pearson Education Limited
Edinburgh Gate, Harlow,
Essex CM20 2JE, England
and Associated Companies throughout the World.

This educational edition first published 1996
Eighth impression 2003

Editorial material set in 10/12.5 pt Stone Sans
Printed in Singapore (KHL)

ISBN 0 582 25384 5

The publisher's policy is to use paper manufactured from
sustainable forests.

Acknowledgements

We are grateful to the following for permission to reproduce copyright material.

BBC Enterprises Ltd for an extract from *Pole to Pole* by Michael Palin; the author,
Jimmy Boyle for extracts from *The Pain of Confinement;* Falling Wall Press Ltd for
extracts from *Nella Last's War* by Nella Last, ed. R Broad and S Fleming (1981); Victor
Gollancz Ltd and the literary executor of Vera Brittain, Paul Berry, and ed. Alan
Bishop, for extracts from *Chronicle of Youth* by Vera Brittain; The Orion Publishing
Group Ltd for an extract from *Diaries* by Alan Clark; Penguin Books Ltd for extracts
from *Zlata's Diary* by Zlata Filipović, translated by Christina Pribichevich-Zoric
(Viking, 1994) copyright Fixot et Editions Robert Laffont, 1993; Random House UK
Ltd for extracts from *Yours, Plum* by P G Wodehouse, ed. F Donaldson; Vallentine
Mitchell & Co. Ltd for an extract from *The Diary of Anne Frank* by Anne Frank
copyright Vallentine Mitchell & Co. Ltd.

We are grateful to Zafer Baran for permission to reproduce the photograph on the
cover.

Cover design by Ship

147

Pre-1914 Collections

Thomas Hardy   *Wessex Tales*   0 582 25405 1
selected by Geoff Barton   *Two Centuries*   0 582 25390 X
                          Stories Old and New   0 582 28931 9
selected by Jane Christopher   *War Stories*   0 582 28927 0
selected by Susie Campbell   *Characters from Pre-20th Century Novels*
                          0 582 25388 8
selected by Celeste Flower   *Diaries and Letters*   0 582 25384 5
selected by Linda Marsh   *Highlights from 19th-Century Novels*
                          0 582 25385 3
                          Landmarks   0 582 25389 6
                          Travel Writing   0 582 25386 1
selected by Tony Parkinson   *Nineteenth-Century Short Stories of Passion and
                          Mystery*   0 582 33807 7

Pre-1914 Poetry

edited by Adrian Tissier   *Poems from Other Centuries*   0 582 22585 X

Pre-1914 Plays

Oliver Goldsmith   *She Stoops to Conquer*   0 582 25397 7
Henrik Ibsen   *Three Plays*   0 582 24948 1
Christopher Marlowe   *Doctor Faustus*   0 582 25409 4
selected by Linda Marsh   *Starting Shakespeare*   0 582 28930 0
Bernard Shaw   *The Devil's Disciple*   0 582 25410 8
                Arms and the Man   0 582 07785 0
John Webster   *The Duchess of Malfi*   0 582 28731 6
Oscar Wilde   *The Importance of Being Earnest*   0 582 07784 2